# How to Deal with Conflict Book

CRAFTED BY SKRIUWER

**Copyright © 2024 by Skriuwer.**

All rights reserved. No part of this book may be used or reproduced in any form whatsoever without written permission except in the case of brief quotations in critical articles or reviews.

At **Skriuwer**, we're more than just a team—we're a global community of people who love books. In Frisian, "Skriuwer" means "writer," and that's at the heart of what we do: creating and sharing books with readers worldwide. Wherever you are in the world, **Skriuwer** is here to inspire learning.

**Frisian** is one of the oldest languages in Europe, closely related to English and Dutch, and is spoken by about **500,000 people** in the province of **Friesland** (Fryslân), located in the northern Netherlands. It's the second official language of the Netherlands, but like many minority languages, Frisian faces the challenge of survival in a modern, globalized world.

We're using the money we earn to promote the Frisian language.

For more information, contact : **kontakt@skriuwer.com** (www.skriuwer.com)

# TABLE OF CONTENTS

## CHAPTER 1: UNDERSTANDING CONFLICT

- Conflict is a natural part of life and can lead to better understanding when approached correctly.
- Differentiates small, everyday conflicts from deeper, long-term disputes.
- Emphasizes that conflict itself is not negative—it's how we respond that matters.

## CHAPTER 2: TYPES OF CONFLICT

- Highlights various categories: internal, interpersonal, and group conflicts.
- Shows how misunderstandings, unmet needs, or power struggles can cause disagreements.
- Suggests identifying the conflict type to choose the right solution path.

## CHAPTER 3: CONFLICT AND EMOTIONS

- Examines how emotions like anger, sadness, or fear drive conflict behavior.
- Underscores recognizing and naming feelings to avoid explosive reactions.
- Recommends strategies for calmly expressing emotions in disagreements.

## CHAPTER 4: HEALTHY COMMUNICATION

- Explains clear, honest speaking and active listening as pillars of resolving disputes.
- Gives tips for using polite language, tone & clear organization when addressing issues.
- Stresses fairness and empathy in conversation to minimize conflict.

## CHAPTER 5: LISTENING SKILLS

- Defines the difference between hearing and active listening.
- Offers techniques to show genuine interest, such as asking clarifying questions and summarizing points.
- Highlights how good listening can defuse tension and prevent misunderstandings.

## CHAPTER 6: SPEAKING SKILLS

- Focuses on calm, respectful ways to share your viewpoint, even when upset.
- Introduces "I" statements and avoiding blame language to keep dialogue constructive.
- Shows how clear speaking can reduce defensiveness and open paths to agreement.

## CHAPTER 7: FINDING COMMON GROUND

- Encourages seeking shared interests or goals rather than fixating on disagreements.
- Demonstrates how to identify deeper needs behind surface conflicts.
- Illustrates that mutual benefits or compromise can unify opposing sides.

## CHAPTER 8: PROBLEM-SOLVING STEPS

- Provides a structured framework for conflict resolution: define the problem, gather info, brainstorm, evaluate, and implement.
- Emphasizes fairness, clarity, and follow-up to ensure lasting solutions.
- Recommends staying calm throughout each phase.

## CHAPTER 9: CONFLICT AT HOME

- Examines common family disputes over chores, personal space, and roles.
- Suggests family meetings, consistent rules, and empathy among members.
- Advises on handling power differences and sibling rivalry with respect.

## CHAPTER 10: CONFLICT AT SCHOOL

- Covers peer disagreements, teacher-student issues, and group project tensions.
- Promotes inclusivity, fairness, and peer mediation programs.
- Proposes calm, step-by-step discussions to keep school conflicts from growing.

## CHAPTER 11: CONFLICT WITH FRIENDS

- *Analyzes loyalty, trust, and jealousy as common triggers.*
- *Teaches honest, gentle conversations to maintain strong bonds.*
- *Emphasizes forgiveness and boundary-setting when necessary.*

## CHAPTER 12: CONFLICT AT WORK

- *Identifies workplace stressors like workload imbalances, office politics, and power struggles.*
- *Recommends professional mediation, clear roles, and transparent communication.*
- *Stresses leadership's role in fostering a respectful office culture.*

## CHAPTER 13: RESPECT AND EMPATHY

- *Presents respect as recognizing another's worth and empathy as understanding their feelings.*
- *Shows how both traits reduce blame and promote healthier solutions.*
- *Highlights consistent respectful behavior as a key to de-escalating conflicts.*

## CHAPTER 14: HANDLING ANGER

- *Explores anger as a normal reaction that can become harmful if uncontrolled.*
- *Offers practical de-escalation tools like deep breathing and time-outs.*
- *Illustrates expressing anger constructively rather than suppressing or exploding.*

## CHAPTER 15: SELF-CONTROL STEPS

- *Shows how pausing, setting goals, and recognizing triggers build stronger self-control.*
- *Suggests practicing daily discipline in small tasks to prepare for bigger conflicts.*
- *Links personal boundaries and calm responses to better outcomes in disagreements.*

## CHAPTER 16: CALMING DOWN IN TENSE TIMES

- *Features immediate techniques to lower tension.*
- *Describes calming strategies for different situations—home, work, public.*
- *Underlines the power of calm leadership or facilitation to ease group stress.*

## CHAPTER 17: ASKING FOR SUPPORT

- *Explains when and how to seek outside help from friends, counselors, or mediators.*
- *Encourages overcoming shame or fear of judgment to receive emotional or professional guidance.*
- *Highlights support as a sign of strength, not weakness.*

## CHAPTER 18: POSITIVE CHANGE FROM CONFLICT

- *Shows how disagreements can spark improvements in families, workplaces, or communities.*
- *Reflects on conflict as a catalyst for policy changes or personal growth.*
- *Emphasizes viewing tension as an opportunity for learning and innovation.*

## CHAPTER 19: KEEPING PEACE IN GROUPS

- *Focuses on group dynamics, from preventing cliques to addressing leadership challenges.*
- *Offers structures like fair rules, inclusive decision-making, and emotional safety to maintain harmony.*
- *Demonstrates early-warning signs of group conflicts and how to resolve them quickly.*

## CHAPTER 20: LOOKING AHEAD TO ONGOING HARMONY

- *Summarizes key conflict resolution tools for long-term use across different life areas.*
- *Stresses adapting to new challenges, continuous self-reflection, and balanced relationships.*
- *Encourages embracing conflict as part of growth and staying aligned with core values.*

# Chapter 1: Understanding Conflict

Conflict is a normal part of life. It happens when people disagree or want different things. Sometimes, conflict can feel scary because we do not know how it will end. Other times, conflict can be simple and quick to fix. It can even have helpful results, because it can make us learn about each other's wishes and ideas. When we think about conflict, we might see people arguing, refusing to speak, or feeling upset. These actions happen when people do not agree. Still, conflict is not always bad. The way we respond to conflict matters more than the conflict itself. If we know how to handle it in a healthy way, conflict can lead to better understanding between people.

Every person faces conflict at some time. It might happen in a home, at school, among friends, or anywhere else. For example, two classmates might argue about who gets to use certain markers. Or two friends might disagree on how to spend their day. Even if these problems seem small, they can create strong feelings. People might feel angry, sad, or stressed. By understanding what conflict is, we can learn how to manage it instead of letting it get out of control.

One reason conflict occurs is that each person has unique experiences and beliefs. We might each think our way is best. Sometimes, we do not listen closely to what others say. Other times, we might ignore how the other person feels. These behaviors make disagreements grow. When people see that their needs or wants do not match, a conflict can arise. For example, you might want to go outside to play, but your sibling wants to stay indoors and watch a show. If both of you must share a single TV and cannot agree on how to use your free time, a conflict can begin. Recognizing this early can help you find a fair solution.

Small conflicts and big conflicts work a bit differently. A small conflict might be deciding who takes the last slice of pizza. A bigger conflict might involve deep disagreements about how a family shares chores or money. Big conflicts can last a long time and can hurt relationships. People may stop trusting or liking each other if the conflict goes on without a solution. Smaller conflicts are often easier to handle, but even small ones can grow if we let them. Watching for signs of conflict can help us handle it when it is still small. Then it will not become something harder to fix.

Some people see conflict as a sign that one side is wrong and the other side is right. But conflict is not always about who is correct. Often, both sides have reasons for their views. For instance, you might argue with a friend about which movie to watch. Each person might have good points. One might want something funny, while the other wants something exciting. Both reasons can be valid. Trying to see the other side can help reduce tension. When we step back to look at both points of view, we might come up with an option that includes parts of each idea.

Feelings can be very strong when there is a disagreement. People might feel fear, anger, or shame. Some try to hide these feelings, which can make them grow stronger. Later, they might explode in anger or leave without solving anything. Recognizing these feelings is a big part of understanding conflict. If we feel upset, we can try to calm ourselves first. Then we can speak about the conflict more clearly. Telling others how we feel can also help them see our side better. It might keep a small conflict from turning into a big, hurtful argument.

There is another side to conflict that can be helpful. Sometimes, conflict alerts us that something needs to change. It can point out a plan or behavior that no longer works for everyone. For example, if you argue every night with your sibling about who washes dishes, maybe the chore plan is not fair. The conflict helps you notice this. Then you can work together to make a new plan. Without the conflict, you might never fix the problem. In this way, conflict can bring needed changes. The key is to stay respectful and open-minded when looking for answers.

Respect is important in all disagreements. Respect means we see that others matter, too. It means we speak kindly and avoid name-calling, even if we feel angry. Sometimes, when people are upset, they forget respect. They shout or use mean words. This behavior can make the conflict bigger, and it can hurt the other person. Even if the other person is not showing respect first, we can still choose to do so. Keeping a respectful tone can calm the situation. It shows the other side we are willing to talk without harming them. This can encourage them to lower their tone and try to cooperate.

Conflict can feel frightening because it might threaten our sense of safety or belonging. We might worry that people will not like us if we do not do what they want. We might fear losing a friend or being seen as unkind. These worries can cause us to argue more intensely or to shut down. But if we see conflict as a normal part of life, we can learn to handle it without panic. We can look for ways to fix the disagreement instead of fighting to hurt the other person. Even if we cannot solve it completely, we can keep it from harming our relationship too much.

When we understand conflict, we recognize that we have the power to deal with it. We can choose a calm approach or a respectful tone, which can lead to better results. Conflicts can become big or small depending on how we react. If we talk calmly and look for solutions, we have a better chance at peace. If we shout, blame, or ignore the problem, it might become larger. This is why it is good to know what conflict is and how it forms. It allows us to manage it before it grows.

We also need to know that conflict looks different in different places. At home, conflicts might involve personal space, chores, or family schedules. At school, they might involve classmates, projects, or seating arrangements. Among friends, conflict might pop up over shared interests, secrets, or trust. When we understand that each environment can bring its own set of problems, we can be ready to respond in ways that fit each situation. For instance, solving a conflict about chores might involve splitting tasks more evenly, while solving a conflict at school might involve talking to a teacher.

It is also useful to note that conflict can be confused with bullying. Bullying is when someone tries to hurt or control another person on purpose and often does it repeatedly. Conflict is not always like that. Conflict is usually a disagreement or a clash of ideas, not a plan to harm someone. It is important to tell the difference. If someone is bullying you, you should talk to a trusted adult for help. If it is a normal conflict, you might work it out by talking or by using the steps you learn in this book. Understanding these differences makes conflict feel more manageable.

Some conflicts build up over time. They might start small and then grow because nobody addresses them. For example, a friend might tease you gently every day, not realizing it hurts your feelings. You might ignore it at first, but after a while, it starts to bother you more and more. One day, you might snap and say something harsh. The friend, who did not know how much the teasing upset you, might feel surprised or hurt. This kind of conflict could have been avoided by speaking up earlier. Recognizing that small annoyances can turn into bigger conflicts helps us see why we should address problems as soon as they arise.

People also handle conflict in different ways. Some try to win the conflict by being louder or more forceful. Others avoid conflict by staying silent or walking away. Some people look for compromise right from the start, hoping to please everyone. Some might agree quickly just to keep peace, but then feel unhappy later. Understanding your own style can help you see what works and what does not. For instance, if you always avoid conflict, you might never get your needs met. If you always try to win, others might feel intimidated and stop wanting to talk. Finding a balanced approach is best.

Conflict can be shaped by our background. If you grew up in a home where people shouted a lot, you might think yelling is the normal way to handle conflict. Someone else might come from a home where nobody talks about problems at all, so they might hide their feelings. When these two people disagree, each might feel confused by how the other acts. Recognizing the role of background helps us be more patient. We see that people bring their past experiences into the present conflict. If we talk openly about these differences, we can find better ways to settle our disagreements.

Sometimes, we fear conflict because we do not want to upset those we care about. We might give in all the time or ignore our own needs. This can lead to frustration inside ourselves, which might spill out in anger later. On the other hand, some people are not afraid to argue about every little thing, which can also create stress for others. A more balanced way is to accept that conflict will happen sometimes, but we can handle it with calm words and respectful actions. This reduces the fear factor and shows us that disagreements do not have to ruin relationships.

It helps to remember that most conflicts, even big ones, can be solved if people are willing to talk and make changes. Sometimes, it requires outside help, like a teacher, counselor, or parent. But even then, the first step is understanding that conflict is normal. Running away or ignoring the problem may make us feel safe for a moment, but it does not fix anything. Sooner or later, the same issue might come back. By learning to face conflicts bravely, we learn skills that can help us in many parts of life, including future jobs and friendships.

Understanding conflict also means seeing our own part in it. We might blame the other person, saying, "They started it," or, "They are being mean." While that can be true, we still have power over our behavior. We can choose to remain calm or become loud. We can decide to keep listening or cut the other person off. Sometimes, when we stay calm, the other person might calm down too. Even if they do not, we know we did our part to keep things from getting worse. This sense of control can make conflict less scary.

Conflicts often happen because someone said or did something hurtful, even if they did not intend to hurt. Misunderstandings can also spark problems. Maybe we thought a friend said something rude, but they were just joking in a bad way. Maybe we missed a message or did not answer in time, causing someone to feel ignored. If we keep in mind that not all conflict starts with bad intentions, we might approach disagreements with an open mind. We can ask questions to clarify the situation before reacting with anger or frustration.

Finally, understanding conflict prepares us to learn ways to solve it. Conflict resolution skills will be covered in later chapters, where we will talk about listening, speaking, and keeping calm. For now, it is enough to see conflict as a normal event that we can handle in respectful ways. This changes how we feel about disagreements. Instead of seeing them as scary or hopeless, we can see them as chances to fix problems and learn about each other. We do not have to like conflict, but we can face it more confidently once we understand what it is.

We can notice conflict in many areas of our lives—home, school, friendships, and beyond. Each conflict may look different, but they share some basic traits: different needs, different ideas, and strong feelings. When we see these traits, we can say, "Okay, this is a conflict," and begin to use the right tools to address it. By staying respectful, being aware of our feelings, and trying to understand the other side, we build a strong base for good conflict management.

As we move forward in this book, we will look at how emotions shape conflict, how listening matters, and how to speak in ways that do not make conflict bigger. We will also look at ways to stay calm when arguments heat up. The main point is that conflict is part of life, but it does not have to ruin our day or our relationships. By seeing it as something we can manage, we take away some of its power. We feel more in control. That is why understanding conflict is the first important step.

# Chapter 2: Types of Conflict

People often think of conflict as one big idea, but there are actually many types of conflict. They can differ based on who is involved, what the argument is about, and how long it lasts. Learning about these types can help us recognize what we are dealing with and plan how to solve it. Some conflicts are inside our own heads, while others involve two people or even a whole group. Sometimes, the problem is about sharing things, while other times it is about strong beliefs or values. By understanding these differences, we gain a better idea of why conflicts happen and how we can address them.

One type is **internal conflict**, which occurs inside a person. For example, you might feel torn between telling the truth to a friend or hiding it to protect their feelings. Nobody else is arguing with you, yet you still feel stressed or upset. This is because two parts of you are pulling in different directions. Internal conflicts can be challenging because we cannot blame someone else. We have to figure out which path is best. Sometimes, writing down our thoughts or speaking with a trusted friend or adult can help us manage internal conflict.

Another type is **interpersonal conflict**, which involves two people who disagree. This can include you and a sibling arguing over who uses the TV or you and a friend who have different ideas about which game to play. Interpersonal conflicts are very common because people often want different things. They can also be among the easiest to solve, as long as both people are ready to listen. With only two people involved, it can be simpler to talk it out and find a fair answer. But if each person is too upset or unwilling to compromise, the conflict might become bigger.

Conflicts involving a larger number of people are called **group conflicts**. This happens when a group of people disagrees with another group, or when there is a disagreement inside a single group. For example, a group project in school might have members arguing about how to finish a task. Or a sports team might split into sides about who should start the match. Group conflicts can be more complicated than conflicts between just two people, because you have to consider many opinions and feelings. It might take more time to find a solution, and sometimes you need a leader or a mediator to help guide the conversation.

Sometimes, conflicts happen over **resources**, which means items or benefits that people want but do not have enough of to share freely. For instance, if there is one computer at home and two people need it at the same time, they might argue over who gets it. Conflicts over resources can also appear at school, like when a group wants to use certain art supplies but another group needs them, too. Finding a fair way to share resources is key to solving these problems. Taking turns, setting time limits, or finding another resource can help.

Conflicts can also revolve around **power**. This is when people want to be in charge or have control over a situation. For example, in a group project, two classmates might want to be the leader and not want to share that role. Power struggles can lead to a lot of tension because people might feel that being in control makes them important. They may not want to give it up. One way to solve power conflicts is to create clear rules about how decisions are made or to share leadership tasks so that everyone feels included.

Another common type is **value conflict**, which happens when people have different ideas about right and wrong or about what is important in life. For instance, you might believe that telling the truth is always best, while your friend might think it is okay to tell a small lie if it keeps someone from feeling hurt. When these beliefs clash, conflict can arise. Value conflicts can be deep because people do not want to give up what they truly believe. Sometimes, the only solution is to accept that you disagree and not force the other person to change their values. Other times, you might find common ground if you see that your values share some similarities.

Conflicts can also stem from **unmet needs**. Everyone has needs, both physical (food, water, shelter) and emotional (love, respect). If people think they are not getting what they need, they might act out. For instance, a teen might feel they do not get enough attention at home and start to argue with family members to be noticed. Or a child might feel they are not respected by their peers, which can lead to fights. When we realize a conflict is about unmet needs, we can look for ways to meet those needs rather than just focusing on the surface argument.

There are also short-term and long-term conflicts. A **short-term** conflict might appear suddenly and be resolved just as fast, like a quick argument over who sits where at lunch. A **long-term** conflict can last for weeks or months. It might resurface every time certain people talk. These longer conflicts can be more stressful because the feelings keep building. People might bring up old grudges over and over. Recognizing if a conflict is short or long-term helps us decide how much time and effort we need to fix it.

Another angle is to look at conflicts caused by **misunderstandings**. These happen when communication fails. Maybe someone sends a text that seems rude when they were just being brief. Or someone misses a meeting because they wrote down the wrong time. Misunderstandings can lead to arguments if people assume the worst about each other. Realizing that a conflict might just be based on poor communication can help clear things up quickly. Asking questions like, "Did you mean to sound upset?" or, "Could there have been a mistake?" can resolve these conflicts.

Personality conflicts also happen often. **Personality differences** can cause two people to clash even over small things. One person might be very neat, and the other might be comfortable with a bit of mess. If they share a room, they could argue about cleaning. One person might be quiet and the other very talkative, which can also cause friction if they have to work together. Nobody is right or wrong for being who they are, but these differences can create tension if people do not respect each other's style. Finding ways to compromise, like setting rules about shared spaces, can help avoid big arguments.

Changes in life can trigger conflicts, too. People might argue when **roles change**. A child growing older might push for more freedom, while parents still think of them as young. A friend might start hanging out with new people, causing old friends to feel left out. A family move to a new city can create stress and lead to conflict over schedules or chores. Changes can make us feel unsure and lead us to take out our frustration on others. Realizing that change often brings stress can help us handle these conflicts more kindly.

Looking at **group conflicts** in more detail, we see that they can take many shapes. Maybe an entire class wants a certain field trip, but the teacher says the school cannot afford it. Some students might feel cheated, and others might accept the decision. If the group splits into those who protest and those who do not, that can lead to more arguments. Finding ways to talk about group goals, collecting everyone's ideas, and making fair choices can help solve group conflicts. It may take patience, because many people will want to share their thoughts.

We can also classify conflict by how **intense** it is. A minor conflict might be a little disagreement that ends quickly. A moderate conflict could involve more heated words, but people can still discuss it. A severe conflict can cause people to shout or say very hurtful things, and it might even get physical. Knowing how severe a conflict is can help us see if we can handle it ourselves or if we need outside help. A very severe conflict might require the aid of a teacher, counselor, or another person who can set rules and keep everyone safe.

Some conflicts are **public**, happening in front of others. For instance, two classmates might argue loudly in front of the entire class. Public conflicts can cause embarrassment and can pressure people to act tough so they do not look weak. Other conflicts are **private**, happening one-on-one or through private messages. Private conflicts might feel less stressful in terms of an audience, but they can still hurt just as much. They can also feel intense if they happen behind closed doors. Understanding if a conflict is public or private can guide how we choose to fix it. A public argument might need a quiet place to talk. A private one might sometimes benefit from bringing in a neutral person.

Recognizing **patterns** can help us figure out the type of conflict we face most often. Maybe we keep running into conflicts about sharing chores. That suggests a resource conflict. Or perhaps we often clash with a certain friend about right and wrong, which might be a value conflict. By spotting patterns, we can be ready to respond in a more effective way. We can say, "This keeps happening because we never set rules about chores" or, "We have different values, so let's agree to respect each other's views."

Sometimes, conflicts are **mixed**. They might include both personality issues and resource issues. For example, you and your sibling might both want the TV at the same time (a resource conflict), and you might also have different tastes in shows (a preference conflict). You could break this problem into parts: figure out how to share the TV, then think about picking shows. Addressing each part separately can make the conflict easier to solve than if you treat it all as one big mess.

When we know the type of conflict, we can choose the best approach to solve it. If it is an internal conflict, we might talk with someone we trust or write down our thoughts to see them more clearly. If it is interpersonal, we can speak directly to the other person. If it is a group conflict, we might need a group meeting or a fair leader who makes sure everyone gets a turn to speak. If it is about sharing resources, we can set schedules or rules. If it is about values, we might need to accept that we differ and still treat each other with respect.

Seeing the many types of conflict can help us feel less alone. Everyone goes through some kind of conflict, whether it is inside their mind, with another person, or with a group. It is part of life. Knowing this can comfort us when we face a disagreement. It can also remind us to stay patient and respectful. Not every conflict is caused by bad intentions. Sometimes, it is just a clash of needs, wants, or styles.

As this book continues, we will look more closely at how emotions and communication fit into conflict. We will see how listening and speaking in kind ways can keep disagreements from becoming huge problems. But first, it is good to recognize that conflict takes many forms. It can be big or small, simple or complex, private or public, short-term or long-term. People can conflict over resources, power, values, or needs. By naming the conflict we face, we can figure out the right steps to deal with it.

This chapter gives a wide view of the different types of conflict you might see. The next chapters will look at specific tools for handling these conflicts. For now, remember that each type of conflict might need a different answer. What works for a quick misunderstanding might not work for a long-term problem about deep beliefs. What helps two people might not work for a group of ten. Being flexible in how we handle conflict is key.

In short, there is not just one kind of conflict. There are many, each with its own reasons and challenges. Conflicts can be inside ourselves or between us and others. They can involve big groups or small ones. They can be about little items to share or big ideas that shape how we live. By learning these types, we can better spot the conflict we are in and choose a wise path to fix it. This knowledge will help us avoid feeling helpless when a disagreement comes our way. Instead, we will know there is a way forward that respects everyone involved.

# Chapter 3: Conflict and Emotions

Emotions play a large part in any conflict. They guide how we act and speak, and they can make a simple disagreement feel much bigger or more serious. When you are in a conflict, you might feel angry, sad, or afraid. You might feel hurt or embarrassed. These feelings can push you to say or do things you would not normally do. They can also keep you from listening carefully. At the same time, emotions can help you understand what is important to you. They can show you when something is not fair or when you need to stand up for yourself. By learning how emotions affect conflict, you can better control your actions and find calmer ways to resolve problems.

---

**Why Emotions Matter**

Emotions are signals. They tell us that we care about what is happening. For example, if you are angry that a friend broke a promise, this anger might mean that trust is very important to you. If you are sad that a sibling ignores your ideas, it might mean you want to feel valued and heard. When we have strong feelings, it means the conflict touches something we hold dear—whether that is friendship, respect, honesty, or fairness.

However, intense emotions can also cloud our thinking. When we feel very upset, our bodies prepare to defend or escape. We might breathe faster, our hearts may race, and our muscles can tense up. This reaction can be helpful if there is a real danger. But in a normal disagreement, these physical responses can make it hard to talk calmly. Our thoughts might race, and we could say hurtful words. We might not be open to hearing any side but our own. That is why it is so important to recognize emotions before they get out of control.

---

**Common Emotions in Conflict**

- **Anger:** People often feel anger in conflict. Anger can come from feeling treated unfairly or from fear of being harmed. Sometimes anger also appears when we feel embarrassed or disrespected. It is a strong emotion that can push us to argue more aggressively.
- **Sadness:** In some disagreements, we might feel sadness. We might be sad because we think someone we care about no longer respects us, or

because we feel we have lost something important (such as trust or closeness).
- **Fear:** Conflicts can make us afraid of losing a friend or facing punishment. We might also fear that the other person will lash out at us. Fear can cause us to avoid the conflict instead of fixing it.
- **Frustration:** This emotion arises when we feel stuck, like no matter what we say, we cannot get our point across. We might also be frustrated if we think the other person will not give us a chance to explain.
- **Guilt:** Sometimes, we know we made a mistake or did something harmful. We might feel guilty during a conflict, and that guilt can make us act in ways we do not fully understand.
- **Shame:** This is a deep feeling that there is something wrong with us as a person. Conflict can trigger shame if we think we are weak or if someone criticizes who we are. Shame can make us withdraw or become defensive.

These emotions can mix. For instance, we might feel both anger and sadness at the same time. We might feel fear and guilt together. Understanding how these combinations can appear helps us see why conflict can become so confusing.

---

**How Emotions Escalate Conflict**

When we are upset, our reactions can make a small conflict grow. For example, if someone says something that hurts our feelings, we might snap back with an insult. That insult then hurts them, so they might yell or threaten to leave. Soon, a small misunderstanding can spin out of control. In many cases, it is not the actual disagreement but how both sides handle it that creates bigger trouble.

Strong emotions can also cause us to see the worst in others. We might think, "They always do this to me," or, "They never care about what I say." These statements, with words like "always" and "never," can paint the other person as entirely bad. In truth, most people do not act in only one way all the time. But when we are angry or sad, it is easy to forget the bigger picture. This mindset can lead us to say things like, "You always ruin everything," which can cause more harm.

Another way emotions escalate conflict is by making us less willing to listen. If we are too angry, we might only wait for the other person to stop talking so we can shout back. We do not consider their perspective. This lack of listening can lead the other person to feel ignored, which adds to their anger or sadness. Soon, both sides talk past each other without finding any solution. That is how conflicts can continue for a long time.

## Identifying Your Feelings

Before we can handle emotions, we need to know what we are feeling. It sounds simple, but many people have trouble naming their own emotions during a conflict. They might say, "I'm just mad," when they are actually afraid or sad underneath. Learning to be clear about your own feelings can prevent misunderstandings.

1. **Pause and Breathe**: When you notice tension rising, stop for a moment. Take a few slow breaths. This short break can calm your heartbeat and give you a chance to think about what you are feeling.
2. **Ask Yourself Questions**: Think about what is bothering you the most. Is it that you feel disrespected? Are you scared that you might lose something or someone important? Are you angry because you feel left out? Identifying the root cause can help you pinpoint your emotions.
3. **Check Physical Clues**: Our bodies often show how we feel before our minds do. Are your hands shaking? Is your heart pounding? Are you sweating? These clues might point to anger, fear, or stress.
4. **Use Simple Words**: Try labeling your emotion in a straightforward way. For instance, say to yourself, "I feel hurt," or, "I feel embarrassed," or, "I feel angry." By putting a name to it, you become more aware of it.

Doing these steps in the middle of a heated conflict can be hard. But practice can make it simpler. Even if you cannot do it perfectly every time, trying to recognize your feelings helps you move toward a calmer approach.

## Expressing Emotions in a Healthy Way

Once you know how you feel, the next step is to express it without harming the other person or making the conflict worse. You do not have to hide your emotions, but you do want to share them in a way that leads to understanding rather than more fighting.

- **Use "I" Statements**: Instead of saying, "You never listen," try saying, "I feel unheard when I talk, and I wish I could finish my thoughts." This keeps the focus on your feeling rather than blaming the other person.

- **Stay Specific**: Talk about what exactly bothered you. For instance, "I felt upset when you took my notebook without asking," is clearer than, "You always do rude things." Specific points help the other person understand what went wrong.
- **Mind Your Tone**: Shouting or speaking in a sarcastic tone can make others defensive. Even if you feel angry, try to keep your voice steady. If you need a moment to calm down, say something like, "I need a quick break before I can keep talking."
- **Avoid Name-Calling**: Words that shame or insult the other person will worsen the conflict. Even if you are upset, remember that insults close the door to finding a solution.
- **Be Open to Their Feelings**: When you share your emotions calmly, it can encourage the other person to share theirs, too. Listening to each other's feelings might reveal that you both are upset about similar things, like not feeling respected.

### Understanding the Other Person's Feelings

Conflict often involves more than just your own emotions. The other person also has feelings, and they might be just as strong or confusing. If you dismiss their emotions, they might feel worse and become more upset. One key to resolving conflict is to try to see how the other person feels. This does not mean you must agree with them. It just means you recognize that they have their own viewpoint.

1. **Listen Without Interruption**: Let them talk. Even if you disagree, do not jump in too soon. They might have a good reason for their feelings, and hearing them out can calm the situation.
2. **Repeat Back What You Heard**: After they talk, try summarizing what they said: "I hear that you felt left out when I didn't invite you." This shows you care enough to pay attention.
3. **Ask Clarifying Questions**: If something is not clear, ask politely. For example, "Did you feel angry because I was ignoring your messages?" This helps you avoid guesses about their feelings.
4. **Show Empathy**: If it seems they are upset, you can say, "It sounds like that was really hurtful." You do not have to say you are wrong. You are just showing that you understand how they feel.

By validating someone's feelings, you lower their defenses. They see that you are not simply trying to win, but that you want to address the real issue. This can open the door to problem-solving later.

## Managing Emotional Reactions

Sometimes, no matter how hard you try, your feelings might boil over. You might find yourself shaking, crying, or yelling. Or you might freeze and not speak at all. Learning to manage these reactions takes practice. Below are some steps that can help:

- **Take a Break**: If you feel your emotions rising too fast, it is okay to pause the conversation. Ask for a few minutes to step away and calm down. Be sure to agree on a time to come back and finish the talk, so the other person does not feel ignored.
- **Deep Breathing**: Slow, controlled breathing can help your body relax. Inhale slowly for a count of four, hold for a moment, then exhale for a count of four. Repeat this several times.
- **Grounding Exercises**: Focus your attention on something in the present. You might look at an object in the room and describe it in detail. Or place your feet firmly on the ground and notice how they feel. This takes your mind off the strong emotion.
- **Positive Self-Talk**: Remind yourself that you can handle this. Say in your mind, "I can stay calm. We can find a way to talk this through." Encouraging thoughts can steady your mood.
- **Reduce Tension Physically**: Tighten your muscles for a few seconds, then release them. This can help your body relax. Some people also find that holding something cold, like a cold drink, can help them refocus.

These methods might sound simple, but they can make a big difference when tempers are high. The goal is not to ignore your feelings but to slow them down enough so you can speak and listen more effectively.

---

## Emotions and Long-Term Conflicts

In some conflicts, emotions build over time. You might have small clashes over many days or weeks, and each clash adds more hurt or anger. These emotions can pile up, making even a minor comment set off a big outburst. Here are some steps to handle long-term conflict that involves strong emotions:

- **Acknowledge Past Hurt**: If you have had many arguments with the same person, there might be old feelings that never got resolved. Let them know you recognize that the past still affects how you both feel.

- **Discuss Patterns**: Notice if there is a cycle. Maybe you argue whenever you talk about household chores. Maybe you feel upset when they bring up a certain topic. Naming the pattern can help you avoid falling into it without thinking.
- **Seek Outside Help**: For long-term conflicts that produce very strong emotions, you might need a neutral person, such as a counselor or a mediator, to guide the conversation. This is not a failure; it is a wise way to handle a very complicated problem.
- **Set Time Limits on Arguments**: In some situations, people go in circles for hours without progress. Limiting the talk to a set time can help each side stay on track and not exhaust each other with repeated points.
- **Plan Breaks**: If you know emotions run high, agree in advance that either side can request a short break if tension rises too much. This prevents saying things in anger that you might regret later.

---

**Cultural and Family Influences on Emotions**

The way we handle emotions in conflict can come from our upbringing or culture. In some families, people might raise their voices often, and it is considered normal. In others, everyone might speak softly, and showing anger openly is frowned upon. Similarly, in some cultures, it is polite to be very direct, while in others, it is seen as rude. Understanding these differences can help you see why some conflicts get emotional faster. If you and the person you disagree with come from different backgrounds, you might have different ideas about what is respectful or how to show feelings.

It can help to talk about these differences. For example, you might say, "In my home, we usually talk very loudly when we're upset. I realize that might sound angry to you when I'm really just stressed." Or, "I'm used to avoiding direct eye contact when I'm upset, but I see that might come across as ignoring you." Sharing such thoughts can reduce confusion. This does not mean you have to act exactly like them, but understanding each other's norms can lower emotional misunderstandings.

---

**When Emotions Overwhelm Us**

In some conflicts, emotions get so strong that we might cry uncontrollably, yell, or feel like we cannot continue. This can be scary for everyone involved. If you reach this point, it is crucial to stop pushing yourself or the other person to keep talking in that moment. Nobody can think or speak clearly when they feel overwhelmed. Steps you can take if you or the other person becomes overwhelmed include:

1. **Suggest a Pause**: Calmly say, "I'm getting too upset. Can we pause and continue later?" This shows you are not running away but just need space to calm down.
2. **Find a Safe Space**: If you are somewhere tense (like a crowded hallway), move to a quieter spot. Or, if you can, step outside for fresh air. A change of place can help ease the emotional load.
3. **Try Relaxation Techniques**: Use deep breathing, count to ten slowly, or do a simple activity like walking or stretching. Focus on returning your body and mind to a calmer state.
4. **Write Down Feelings**: If talking is too hard, you could write a short note about what you want to say. This gives you time to sort through your emotions without interruption.

Returning to the conflict after such a break might make both of you more willing to talk reasonably. Sometimes, just knowing that you have the option to pause can keep the emotions from getting out of hand.

---

**Conflict Styles Tied to Emotions**

People's emotional responses often match their general style of handling conflict:

- **Avoiders**: They might feel fear or anxiety and try to dodge any confrontation. Their emotions lead them to stay silent.
- **Confronters**: They might feel anger strongly and jump into any conflict head-on, wanting a quick resolution or a "win."
- **Peacemakers**: They might feel worry about losing relationships, so they try to fix problems right away or agree to almost anything to keep the peace.
- **Negotiators**: They feel tension but try to talk it through step by step. They may not always be calm, but they work to balance emotions and logic.

These styles are not fixed forever. People can act differently in various situations. Recognizing your style can help you see why you feel certain emotions in conflict. For example, if you tend to avoid conflict, your anxiety might be high whenever a disagreement arises. Understanding this can help you cope with the stress. Or if you rush into conflict with anger, knowing you do that can help you pause before speaking.

---

**Emotional Safety**
One part of handling conflict well is creating a sense of emotional safety for yourself and the other person. Emotional safety means that both of you can share honestly without fear of being mocked, insulted, or judged harshly. When people feel emotionally safe, they are more likely to open up, listen, and work toward a solution.

How to build emotional safety in a conflict:

1. **Agree to Respectful Rules**: For instance, you can say, "Let's not yell or call names. If we feel too upset, we can take a short break."
2. **Show Willingness to Hear**: Use friendly body language. Try to keep an open posture, no crossed arms or glaring looks. This signals that you are not attacking.
3. **Stay Truthful**: Do not lie or exaggerate to gain an advantage. If the other person catches you bending facts, they will trust you less.
4. **Keep the Focus on the Present Issue**: Avoid bringing up old, unrelated arguments that can make the situation more complicated. Stick to the current problem.
5. **Apologize if Needed**: If you realize you said something hurtful, a simple "I'm sorry I said that. I was upset, but I should not have used those words," can go a long way to restoring safety.

These steps might feel awkward at first if you are not used to them, but they can reduce tension and help keep emotions in check.

---

**Children and Adult Conflicts**
Emotions can run high in conflicts between children and adults. Kids might feel they lack power, and adults might feel responsible for discipline. Understanding

each other's emotional point of view can help. If you are a child, calmly telling an adult how you feel might help them see your side. If you are an adult, listening closely without judgment can make a child feel safe. Both sides must remember that respect is a two-way street. High emotions from either side can stop good communication from happening.

---

**Seeing Emotions as Clues**
It might help to think of emotions as clues or signals, rather than problems. When someone is upset, it often means something they care about is at risk. If your sibling is angry that you borrowed their shirt without asking, that anger is a clue that they value their belongings and privacy. If your friend is sad that you did not call them, that sadness is a clue they value your attention and friendship. When you treat emotions like clues, you can ask, "What need or value is behind this feeling?" That question can guide you to a better solution than just dismissing the emotion as "too big" or "dramatic."

---

**Practical Example**
Imagine you and your friend, Alex, have a conflict because Alex told a secret you shared. You find out and feel angry and betrayed. Your anger boils, and you confront Alex in front of others. Alex feels embarrassed and snaps back at you, saying you never told them it was a secret. Both of you storm away, furious.

A few hours later, you decide to calm down. You breathe deeply, then think about how you actually feel. You realize it is not just anger; you also feel hurt because you trusted Alex and did not expect this. You approach Alex later in private and say, "I felt really hurt when you shared my information. I was angry because I trusted you to keep it between us." You do not point fingers by saying, "You always do this." Instead, you focus on your feelings.

Alex, now less embarrassed, can see why you are upset. They might say, "I'm sorry. I didn't realize it was a secret. I just thought it was normal news." You ask for clarity: "Why didn't you check with me first?" They admit they thought you would not mind. You both realize there was a misunderstanding. You agree that, going forward, Alex will ask before sharing any personal details, and you will be clearer about what is private. In this example, both sides used emotions as clues—hurt showed a need for trust, embarrassment showed a need for understanding. By talking about these feelings calmly, you resolved the conflict.

# Chapter 4: Healthy Communication

Communication is the key to handling conflict well. When we communicate in a healthy way, we share our thoughts and feelings without causing harm. We also listen to the other person and try to see their point of view. Good communication can stop a small conflict from growing and can help fix bigger ones. It is not always easy, especially when emotions are involved. Still, learning basic skills can make a big difference in how we manage disagreements.

---

**What Is Healthy Communication?**

Healthy communication means we speak honestly and kindly, and we listen with an open mind. It involves:

1. **Clarity**: We say exactly what we mean, using simple words that do not confuse the other person.
2. **Respect**: We treat the other person's ideas and feelings as important, even if we do not agree with them.
3. **Listening**: We do not just wait for our turn to speak; we actually hear what the other person says.
4. **Fairness**: We avoid blaming, shaming, or threatening. We focus on solving the problem together.

When we communicate in this way, we reduce misunderstandings. We also create an atmosphere where everyone feels safer to share. People are less likely to explode in anger or walk away in silence if they believe their words will be treated with respect.

---

**Common Barriers to Good Communication**

Sometimes, even when we want to communicate well, we run into problems. Here are a few common barriers:

- **Assuming**: We assume we know what the other person thinks or feels without asking. This can lead to wrong conclusions.
- **Interrupting**: If we cut the other person off, they might feel disrespected. We also miss the chance to hear their full point.

- **Using Vague Language**: Words like "always" or "never" can be too broad. The other person might feel attacked.
- **Letting Emotions Take Over**: Strong feelings can cause yelling or name-calling, which breaks down communication.
- **Mind Reading**: We expect others to know what we want or feel without us telling them. If they fail to guess, we blame them.

Recognizing these barriers can help us avoid them. When you catch yourself interrupting, for example, you can apologize and let the other person continue.

---

**Building Your Message**

Before speaking in a conflict, it helps to think about what you want to say. Planning your words can keep you from blurting out something harmful. Here is a simple way to build your message:

1. **Describe the Situation**: State what happened. For example, "Yesterday, I noticed you closed the door while I was still talking."
2. **Share Your Feelings**: Say how this made you feel. "I felt hurt and ignored."
3. **Explain Why**: Give a reason or context. "I was trying to show you something I worked on for a long time, and it mattered to me."
4. **State What You Need**: Ask for a change or a solution. "Next time, can you let me finish before you walk out, or let me know if it's a bad time to talk?"

This structure keeps the focus on facts, feelings, and needs. It is less likely to sound like an attack. The other person can understand your perspective more clearly and respond with their own view.

---

**Active Listening**

Healthy communication is not just about talking clearly; it is also about listening carefully. Active listening means we do our best to really hear and understand the other person. This involves:

- **Eye Contact**: Look at the speaker (if it is culturally acceptable) so they know you are paying attention.
- **Body Language**: Nod or provide small signals that you are following along. Avoid crossing your arms or looking away.

- **No Interruptions**: Wait until they finish speaking. If you think of a question, remember it until they pause.
- **Paraphrasing**: Repeat back what you heard in your own words. For instance, "It sounds like you felt embarrassed when I joked about you in front of our friends."
- **Asking Questions**: If something is unclear, ask questions to get more detail, such as, "When did you start feeling upset?" or, "Could you tell me more about that situation?"

Active listening shows respect. It also helps prevent miscommunication, because you confirm you heard them correctly. When the other person feels heard, they are often more open to hearing your side as well.

---

### Choosing the Right Time and Place

The timing and location of a discussion can affect how well you communicate. If one person is stressed, tired, or rushed, they might not communicate well. If the setting is noisy or filled with other people, it might be hard to focus. Here are some tips:

1. **Pick a Calm Moment**: If possible, wait until both sides are not in the middle of something else.
2. **Find a Quiet Spot**: A private or semi-private place can help both sides feel more comfortable sharing personal feelings.
3. **Limit Distractions**: Turn off or put away phones, pause music or TV, and ask not to be interrupted.
4. **Be Respectful of Their Schedule**: Do not force a conversation if the other person is about to leave or is busy. Suggest a better time, like, "Could we talk after dinner?"

Sometimes, you cannot control the timing or place. Conflicts can arise suddenly. Even then, you can do your best to move the discussion somewhere quieter or agree to talk in detail later.

---

### Nonverbal Cues

Communication is not just words. Our faces, hands, and posture send messages too. Nonverbal cues can either match what we say or go against it. For example, saying "I'm listening" while rolling your eyes tells the other person you do not respect what they are saying. Here are some helpful nonverbal cues:

- **Open Posture**: Keep your arms relaxed and avoid turning away.
- **Calm Facial Expressions**: Even if you feel tense, try to keep your expression neutral or caring.
- **Gentle Gestures**: Small nods or a soft smile can encourage the other person to keep speaking.
- **Appropriate Space**: Stand or sit at a respectful distance, not too close to crowd them or too far to seem distant.

When your words and your body language match, the other person is more likely to trust your message. If you say you understand but your face shows anger, they might doubt you.

---

### Being Aware of Tone

Tone of voice can change how words are understood. You could say the same phrase in a calm tone or a mocking tone, and it would mean two different things. Pay attention to:

1. **Volume**: Speaking too loudly can seem aggressive. Speaking too softly might seem like you are not confident or that you do not want to talk.
2. **Speed**: Talking very fast can make you sound anxious or impatient. Talking very slowly might sound like you are talking down to the other person.
3. **Attitude**: A sarcastic or sneering tone can upset others, even if your words seem polite.

If you notice your tone shifting due to anger or annoyance, pause and take a breath. It might help you reset and speak more kindly.

---

### Handling Criticism

At times, communication in conflict will include criticism. Someone might say something about your actions or attitude that stings. Healthy communication does not mean never criticizing; sometimes we need to address problematic behavior. However, how we do it matters:

- **Focus on the Behavior, Not the Person**: Say, "I don't like it when you interrupt me," instead of, "You are such a rude person."
- **Give Reasons**: Explain why the behavior is a problem, so the other person understands your point. For example, "When you interrupt me, I lose my train of thought."
- **Suggest Solutions**: If possible, propose what could be done differently next time, such as, "Can you let me finish my sentence and then respond?"

If you are on the receiving end of criticism, try not to become defensive right away. Listen to the words and see if there is truth to them. You can ask questions to clarify. Even if you do not agree fully, acknowledging their view can reduce tension.

---

**The Role of Questions**

Questions can steer a conversation in a productive way if used wisely. Rather than just stating your opinion, ask things like, "How do you see the situation?" or, "What do you think would make this fair for both of us?" These open-ended questions invite the other person to share more details. They also show that you care about what they think. Avoid questions that sound like accusations, such as, "Why are you always so difficult?" or "When will you stop being so stubborn?" Those will only cause more defensiveness.

---

**Dealing with Silence**

Sometimes, the other person refuses to speak or gives very short answers. They might feel scared, angry, or overwhelmed. Or they might not be ready to talk yet. In healthy communication, it is important to respect silence while also offering a chance to speak. You could say, "I notice you're quiet. If you need time to gather your thoughts, we can pause and talk when you feel ready." This shows you recognize their feelings. It also gives them space without pressuring them to respond immediately.

---

**Communicating in Groups**

When there are more than two people involved, healthy communication can be harder. Multiple people might want to talk at once, and some might feel left out. A few guidelines can help:

1. **Establish a Simple Rule**: Only one person speaks at a time.
2. **Use a Time Limit**: Give each person a short amount of time to share their view without interruption.
3. **Stay on Topic**: Keep track of the main issue. If someone brings up something unrelated, gently remind them to return to the original problem.
4. **Have a Neutral Facilitator**: In more serious group conflicts, a neutral person can guide the discussion so nobody dominates or feels ignored.

Group communication requires patience and structure. If everyone follows the same rules, it is easier to hear each voice and work toward a common understanding.

---

## Digital Communication

In today's world, much of our communication happens through text messages, emails, or social media. Conflict can arise or get worse in digital spaces because it is easy to misunderstand tone or intent. Here are some pointers:

- **Wait Before Responding**: If you get an upsetting message, take a moment to cool down. Do not reply in anger.
- **Use Clear Words**: Without body language or tone, words can be read in many ways. Be extra clear about your meaning.
- **Avoid Long Arguments Online**: Complex disagreements are often better handled face-to-face or through a phone call, where each side can hear tone or see facial expressions.
- **Re-Read Before Sending**: Check for any words that might sound harsher than you intended.
- **Seek Clarity**: If something is confusing, ask, "Could you explain what you mean by this?" rather than assuming the worst.

---

## Apologies and Forgiveness

Healthy communication also includes knowing how to apologize when we are wrong and how to accept apologies when offered. A good apology is clear and sincere. It should include:

- **Admitting What You Did**: "I yelled at you and said hurtful things."
- **Saying You Are Sorry**: "I'm truly sorry for how I acted."
- **Stating How You Will Change**: "Next time, I will try to speak calmly or ask for a break if I feel angry."
- **Avoiding Excuses**: Do not say, "I'm sorry, but you made me mad." That puts blame on the other person instead of taking responsibility.

When receiving an apology, try to listen to it fully. If you sense they are sincere, consider forgiving them. Forgiveness does not mean forgetting what happened right away, but it means you are willing to move forward without holding a grudge. If you find it hard to forgive, you can say, "I appreciate your apology, but I need some time to heal."

---

**Long-Term Communication Habits**

Developing healthy communication is not a single event; it is a practice you keep building over time. Here are some habits to keep:

1. **Regular Check-Ins**: With people you often see, check in about how things are going. This might stop small issues from growing into big conflicts.
2. **Seek Feedback**: Ask trusted friends or family how you come across in conflicts. They might notice if you talk too much or interrupt often.
3. **Be Open to Learning**: Different approaches work for different people. Be willing to adjust your style if you see it is not effective.
4. **Stay Curious**: Remind yourself that you do not know everything about the other person's feelings or experiences. Curiosity can lead to better understanding.

---

**Example of Healthy Communication in Conflict**

Imagine you are in a group project with three classmates. One classmate, Taylor, keeps ignoring your ideas. You feel annoyed and unappreciated. Instead of accusing Taylor in front of everyone, you wait until there is a good moment. You pull Taylor aside and speak calmly:

- **Describe the Situation**: "In our group talks, I noticed that whenever I share an idea, it seems like you move on without responding."
- **Share Your Feelings**: "I feel left out and wonder if my ideas do not matter."
- **Explain Why**: "I have been working hard on my part of the project, and I want to make sure my input is heard."
- **State What You Need**: "Can we make sure we respond to each person's idea before moving on? Maybe we can take turns sharing."

Taylor might be surprised and say, "I didn't realize I was ignoring you. I was just in a hurry to finish." By staying calm and clear, you gave Taylor a chance to explain. Then, you can agree on a plan where each group member has a set time to speak during meetings. This simple step can fix the conflict without anger or blame.

---

**Putting It All Together**

Healthy communication is at the heart of conflict resolution. It helps us speak honestly, listen closely, and find solutions that respect everyone. It takes practice because emotions and misunderstandings can derail a conversation quickly. But by preparing what you want to say, using respectful words, controlling your tone, and truly listening, you can often prevent conflicts from getting worse and sometimes solve them completely.

Here is a short checklist you can keep in mind:

1. **Know Your Goal**: What do you hope to achieve in this conversation?
2. **Plan Your Words**: How can you explain your side clearly and respectfully?
3. **Listen Actively**: Are you giving the other person your full attention?
4. **Stay Aware of Tone and Body Language**: Is your nonverbal communication matching your words?
5. **Offer Solutions**: Can you propose a fix or invite the other person to suggest one?
6. **Remain Flexible**: Be ready to hear new information that could change your mind.
7. **Agree on Next Steps**: Summarize what both sides will do moving forward.

With these steps, you build a healthy communication style that not only helps in conflicts, but also strengthens relationships in general. People will be more willing to work with you, trust you, and open up to you when they see that you treat them and their opinions with fairness and kindness. Healthy communication is not magic—it does not guarantee that every disagreement will go your way or end perfectly. But it does maximize the chance of reaching understanding and peace.

When we choose to communicate in a kind and clear way, we make it easier for everyone to speak up, share concerns, and fix problems together. This lays the foundation for resolving future conflicts before they grow. It also helps maintain respect, even when people do not see eye to eye. By caring about both truth and empathy, we show that we value the relationship, not just the outcome of the argument. This attitude can turn conflicts into productive discussions, and that is what healthy communication is all about.

# Chapter 5: Listening Skills

Listening is more than just hearing words. It involves paying attention, trying to understand the speaker's meaning, and making sure the other person feels heard. When we listen well in a conflict, we show respect and concern for the other person's thoughts. This can reduce anger or stress on both sides. Listening is not always easy, especially when we are upset or have our own ideas we want to share. However, with practice, we can improve our ability to take in what someone else is saying and respond in ways that help solve disagreements rather than add to them.

---

### 1. Why Listening Is So Important

In many conflicts, people focus on what they want to say next. They might prepare their argument in their mind while the other person is still talking. This means they miss key details that could help them understand the full story. Real listening involves pausing our own thoughts and concerns to truly hear the other side.

- **Reduces Tension**: When someone feels heard, they are less likely to shout or behave rudely. Feeling heard can calm strong emotions, making it easier to talk things out.
- **Builds Trust**: Showing that you care enough to listen carefully can create a sense of trust. This is true in families, friendships, and larger groups.
- **Reveals Underlying Issues**: Sometimes, a conflict is about more than the surface disagreement. Perhaps the speaker feels ignored or disrespected in general. By listening, you may uncover deeper reasons behind the conflict.
- **Helps Avoid Misunderstandings**: Misunderstandings often happen when people only catch part of what is said. Listening carefully ensures you get the full message, which reduces confusion.

---

### 2. Hearing vs. Listening

It is common to confuse hearing with listening. Hearing is just the physical act of sound waves hitting our ears. Listening is an active choice. We take the information in, think about it, and try to understand the speaker's intent. Here are some differences:

- **Hearing**: Automatic, requires no focus, can happen even if we are daydreaming or distracted.
- **Listening**: A decision to focus on the speaker, interpret their words, and pick up on tone or feelings.

For instance, if your sibling complains about chores while you are watching a show, you might hear the noise of their voice but not process the details. If you decide to pause the show and turn your full attention to them, you move from hearing to listening.

---

### 3. Levels of Listening
Not all listening happens on the same level. Sometimes, we "sort of" pay attention, and sometimes we listen very carefully.

1. **Pretend Listening**: The person nods or says "uh-huh" but is actually thinking about something else.
2. **Selective Listening**: The listener pays attention only to parts they like or agree with, ignoring the rest.
3. **Active Listening**: The listener focuses completely, asks questions, and tries to understand the whole message.
4. **Empathetic Listening**: This is active listening plus a deeper effort to see the speaker's feelings. The listener tries to step into the other person's shoes.

During conflict resolution, the higher levels of listening (active or empathetic) are most helpful. When both sides try to truly understand each other, it becomes easier to reach solutions that feel fair.

---

### 4. Key Skills for Good Listening
Effective listening is made up of several habits and actions that we can practice every day:

- **Attentive Body Language**: Face the speaker, make gentle eye contact (if appropriate), and keep your body pointed toward them. This signals that you are ready to hear what they say.

- **No Interruptions**: Let the speaker finish their thoughts before responding. If you interrupt, they may feel disrespected or think you value your own words more than theirs.
- **Asking Clarifying Questions**: When you do not understand a point, it is better to ask politely rather than guess. For example, "Can you tell me more about what happened at school?"
- **Reflecting**: Repeat back in your own words what you heard. This confirms you understood and allows the speaker to correct you if needed. For instance, "It sounds like you felt sad because you were left out of the group activity."
- **Avoiding Judgments**: Stay away from labeling the speaker as wrong, silly, or overreacting. Even if you disagree, let them share without cutting them down.
- **Patience**: Some people talk slowly or need a moment to find the right words. Rushing them can cause them to shut down.

---

### 5. Listening for Feelings and Needs

In conflicts, people often have hidden feelings and needs that might not be obvious right away. They might sound angry, but underneath they could be sad or scared. Listening for deeper feelings requires paying attention to tone, body language, and word choices.

- **Clues in Tone**: A quivering voice might mean the speaker is about to cry, indicating sadness or fear. A sharp, loud tone could show anger or frustration.
- **Observing Body Language**: Do they have tense shoulders, a tight jaw, or downcast eyes? These clues can reveal emotions they might not say out loud.
- **Understanding Needs**: If someone keeps repeating a certain theme (like "Nobody respects me"), their deeper need might be for recognition or consideration.
- **Responding with Empathy**: You can say, "I see that you're upset about not being heard. I want to understand more about that." This invites them to open up further.

When we identify the feelings behind the conflict, we can look for solutions that address those deeper needs, not just the surface problem.

## 6. Barriers That Block Listening

Even if we want to be good listeners, certain obstacles can get in the way:

1. **Prejudice or Bias**: If we have a preset opinion about the speaker, we might ignore what they say or twist it to fit our own view.
2. **Emotional Overload**: If we are too angry or upset, it is tough to focus. Our mind might race, or we might only want to defend ourselves.
3. **Noise and Distractions**: External distractions like phone alerts, TV, or other people talking can break our concentration.
4. **Time Pressure**: If we feel rushed, we might push the speaker to wrap up quickly, causing them to feel hurried and misunderstood.
5. **Wanting to Win**: In a heated conflict, we might only listen for flaws in the other person's argument, planning how to counter them instead of trying to understand.

Recognizing these barriers can help us remove or reduce them. For example, if phones distract us, we can set them aside or turn off notifications during a serious conversation.

## 7. Overcoming Roadblocks to Listening

Removing barriers to listening involves a few practical steps:

- **Check Your Mood**: If you feel too angry to listen, pause the discussion or take a deep breath before continuing. A calm mind is more open to hearing.
- **Choose a Good Spot**: Move to a quieter room or area if noise is an issue.
- **Set Aside Bias**: Remind yourself that everyone has their own story, and you might learn something new if you keep an open mind.
- **Use Self-Talk**: If you catch yourself trying to "win" the argument, gently remind yourself, "Right now, I just need to understand their point."
- **Manage Time**: If you are really busy, see if you can reschedule the talk for a better time. If you must talk now, let the other person know you are fully present for as long as you can be.

These small choices can help you become a more focused listener, which in turn makes conflicts easier to navigate.

## 8. Listening in Groups

Group conflicts involve multiple speakers, so listening becomes even more important—and more complicated. If three or more people try to speak at once, nobody feels heard. One approach is to set clear rules:

- **One Speaker at a Time**: Have each person speak without interruption for a set length of time, like one minute.
- **Use a Cue**: Some groups use a small object (like a pencil) that the current speaker holds. Only the person with the pencil can speak, and then they pass it on.
- **Paraphrase Before Replying**: Ask each listener to restate what the speaker said. This ensures no one jumps in with their own point without first showing they listened.
- **Rotate Turns**: Make sure everyone who wants to speak gets a turn. This prevents louder voices from dominating.

These methods can help large groups handle conflicts or disagreements in a fair, organized way.

## 9. Checking for Understanding

In conflict situations, there is a risk of misunderstanding. Even if you listen carefully, you might still interpret something differently from how the speaker intended. Checking for understanding is a step that helps clear up confusion before it causes more trouble.

Ways to check:

- **Summaries**: "I want to make sure I get it right. You're saying that our project deadlines feel too tight, and you want more help, correct?"
- **Encourage Corrections**: "Did I misunderstand any part of that? Please let me know if I did."
- **Ask Detailed Questions**: "When you say you feel ignored, can you tell me a time that happened?"

This process might feel slow, but it saves time and stress later by preventing escalation due to misunderstandings.

## 10. Listening with Empathy in Daily Conflicts

Consider a small daily conflict: your friend is annoyed because you did not message them back as soon as they expected. You might be tempted to say, "I was busy. Why are you overreacting?" But before you react, try empathetic listening:

1. **Give Them Space to Talk**: Let them explain why they are upset. Maybe they had an important issue they needed to discuss.
2. **Ask about Feelings**: "It sounds like you felt let down. Were you worried about something?"
3. **Confirm**: "So, you wanted me to be there for you because you were having a rough day, right?"
4. **Move Forward**: Now that you know they felt unsupported, you can talk about ways to handle future situations, like agreeing on how quickly each of you usually responds.

In this example, your friend might calm down because they see you are making a real effort to understand. Even if you had a good reason for not messaging, showing that you care about their feelings can repair the hurt.

---

## 11. Practical Exercises to Improve Listening

Like any skill, listening improves with practice. Here are a few exercises you can try:

- **Repeat Game**: Have a short conversation with a friend or family member. After they speak for about one minute, repeat what they said as closely as possible. Then switch roles. This helps you focus on the content.
- **Ask 3 Questions**: During a talk, commit to asking three sincere questions about what the other person said. This keeps you engaged and helps you learn more details.
- **Mirror Emotions**: Practice identifying the speaker's emotions by their tone or face, and then name them back. "You seem excited" or "You look worried." If you are wrong, they can correct you.
- **No Device Time**: During important conversations, turn off or silence electronic devices. Set them aside so your full focus is on listening.
- **No Response Practice**: Let someone talk about an issue while you only nod or use short phrases like "I see" for a set time. Try not to give advice or share your own opinion until they finish.

These exercises can feel awkward at first, but they help build stronger listening habits. Over time, you will likely find that you catch more details and respond more thoughtfully.

## 12. Being Mindful and Present

Sometimes the hardest part of listening is staying in the moment. Our minds wander, or we think of what we want to say next. Here are some ways to remain present:

- **Eye Contact** (if comfortable): Looking gently at the speaker can keep you focused on them.
- **Deep Breathing**: If you feel yourself drifting, take a slow breath and bring your attention back to their words.
- **Summarize Internally**: In your mind, repeat a short summary of what the speaker just said. This keeps you from daydreaming.
- **Avoid Multi-Tasking**: Do not check messages or shuffle papers while someone is speaking to you. Finish one thing at a time.

Being mindful helps you not only catch the speaker's words but also pick up on their tone and pace, which give clues about their feelings.

## 13. Encouraging Others to Speak

Sometimes, the other person is shy, nervous, or unsure whether they should share. To encourage them:

1. **Ask Open-Ended Questions**: Questions that need more than a "yes" or "no," such as, "How did you feel about the decision?"
2. **Use Gentle Prompts**: "Would you like to say more about that?"
3. **Show Appreciation**: "Thank you for explaining that. I value your thoughts."
4. **Stay Patient**: If they pause or hesitate, do not jump in right away. Give them a moment to gather their words.

By creating a safe space for them to express themselves, you reduce the risk of misunderstandings later. Even if you disagree, hearing their perspective fully can prevent future conflicts.

## 14. Listening in Conflicts with Authority Figures

Conflicts with teachers, bosses, or parents can feel one-sided, because they have more power in some ways. Still, better listening can help both sides:

- **For the Person with Less Power**: If you are the child or the employee, try to show that you understand the authority figure's expectations. Ask clear questions so they see you are taking their words seriously.
- **For the Authority Figure**: If you are the parent or boss, listening carefully to the other side can show fairness. Repeating their points back can prove you value their input.

In these situations, calm communication can help avoid harsh punishments or feelings of disrespect. It also helps build a relationship based on trust.

## 15. Handling Long or Repetitive Speakers

Some people talk a lot or repeat the same points. This can test our patience. However, if we cut them off rudely, they might feel silenced. Here are some polite strategies:

- **Acknowledge Their Points**: Gently summarize what they have said so they know you are listening. "You've mentioned several times how worried you are about deadlines."
- **Set a Time to Talk**: If you know they will speak for a while, plan a proper time slot. "I have about 15 minutes right now to give you my full attention."
- **Redirect Gently**: If they start repeating themselves, you can say, "I understand your concern about deadlines. Is there anything new you'd like me to know, or should we move on to discussing solutions now?"
- **Maintain Respect**: Even if you feel restless, try not to roll your eyes or let out big sighs. Stay calm and polite.

This way, you show respect while guiding the conversation toward a more productive path. You do not dismiss their words, but you also do not let the conflict stall on one repeated idea.

## 16. The Role of Silence in Listening

Silence can be a powerful part of good listening. Many people rush to fill pauses because they feel uncomfortable. Yet a few seconds of silence can give the speaker time to think and add more detail. It can also let you reflect on what was just said. Some tips for using silence:

- **Count in Your Head**: If the speaker goes quiet, mentally count to three before speaking. They might continue once they gather their thoughts.
- **Stay Relaxed**: Keep a calm posture, so the speaker does not feel pressured.
- **Ask if They Want to Say More**: After a brief pause, you can gently ask, "Is there anything else you'd like me to understand?"
- **Avoid Rapid-Fire Questions**: If you ask too many questions quickly, the speaker may feel hurried and not share fully.

Silence is not always an enemy in conversation. It can be a space that allows deeper thoughts to surface.

---

## 17. When the Other Person Does Not Listen

You might run into a situation where you are trying to listen, but the other person does not do the same for you. They might interrupt, dismiss your points, or refuse to hear you out. While you cannot control their behavior, you can control yours:

- **Stay Polite**: Resist the urge to interrupt back or yell. Show the behavior you wish they would show.
- **Ask Politely for a Turn**: "I'd like to share my thoughts too. Could I have a moment to explain?"
- **Suggest Ground Rules**: If it is a repeated problem, propose guidelines: "Let's give each other two minutes each to speak, then respond."
- **Know When to Pause**: If they are too heated to listen, it may help to pause the talk and try later.

By staying respectful, you keep the door open for healthier communication later. Even if they do not meet you halfway now, you have done your part to keep things calmer.

### 18. Cultural Influences on Listening

Communication styles differ across cultures. In some cultures, people might raise their voices and speak with strong emotion. In others, a quiet or calm tone is seen as the norm. Knowing these differences can help you adjust your listening style. If the speaker is from a background where conversation moves quickly, you might need to stay more alert for clues. If they are from a background that values pauses and slow speech, you might be patient with longer silences. Being aware of these cultural differences can reduce misunderstandings and show respect for the other person's way of speaking.

---

### 19. Listening to Your Own Needs

While listening to others, do not forget to be aware of your own comfort. If you feel overwhelmed, it is okay to ask for a brief break. It is also important to check your energy and emotional state. Effective listening does not mean letting the other person drain you without limit. You can let them know, "I want to keep listening, but I need a quick moment to gather myself." Taking care of yourself allows you to continue being a supportive listener in the long run.

---

### 20. Daily Benefits of Better Listening

Improving your listening skills is not just for conflict resolution. It also:

1. **Strengthens Relationships**: Friends and family will appreciate the care you show when you listen well.
2. **Boosts Learning**: At school or work, good listening helps you learn new information more effectively.
3. **Increases Empathy**: By hearing others' stories, you develop deeper compassion.
4. **Builds Confidence**: When you understand people better, you often feel more at ease in social settings.
5. **Prevents Small Problems from Growing**: Spotting concerns early through active listening can stop them from becoming bigger conflicts.

# Chapter 6: Speaking Skills

Speaking skills help us share our thoughts clearly and respectfully, even when we are upset or disagree with someone. In a conflict, unkind or unclear words can make things worse. On the other hand, well-chosen words can encourage cooperation and reduce hostility. Learning to speak in a calm, focused manner is crucial for solving disagreements in a healthy way. This chapter will explore the elements of effective speaking, common pitfalls, and practical tips to help you express yourself in conflicts without causing more harm.

### 1. Why Speaking Skills Matter in Conflict

When people think of conflict resolution, they often focus on ideas like compromise or negotiation. While those are important, they rely on good speaking and listening. If you cannot communicate your feelings, needs, or suggestions well, others will have trouble understanding you. This can lead to frustration, repeated arguments, or even a complete breakdown in communication. By improving speaking skills, you help others see exactly what you want or need, making it more likely that they will try to find a fair solution with you.

### 2. Speaking vs. Venting

There is a difference between speaking in a productive way and venting. Venting often involves letting out every negative feeling without regard for how the other person will receive it. Productive speaking means you share your emotions and thoughts in a structured and respectful manner. While it might feel good to vent in the moment, it can hurt relationships or escalate the conflict if you say things in an uncontrolled way. Productive speaking still allows you to show hurt or anger, but it is channeled through clear, respectful communication.

### 3. Elements of Clear Speech

Clear speech in conflict includes:

1. **Conciseness**: Try to be direct. If you talk for too long or bring in unrelated issues, the main point can get lost.

2. **Organization**: Present your thoughts in a logical order. For example, start with what happened, then explain why it bothered you, and end with what you want to change.
3. **Respectful Tone**: Even if you are angry, speak in a steady voice. Avoid shouting or heavy sarcasm.
4. **Specific Language**: Use details or examples to avoid confusion. For instance, "You did not show up at 4 PM like we agreed" is clearer than "You never keep your promises."
5. **Polite Manner**: Words like "please," "thank you," and "I appreciate" can keep the mood less tense.

By focusing on these elements, you let the other person see that you want to fix the problem, not just blame them.

---

**4. The Power of "I" Statements**

A common technique for reducing tension in conflicts is to use "I" statements instead of "you" statements. This approach shifts the focus away from attacking the other person and toward expressing your own feelings.

- **"You" Statement Example**: "You are so careless! You never help with cleaning."
- **"I" Statement Example**: "I feel overwhelmed because the kitchen is a mess, and I need your help to keep it clean."

By saying "I feel" or "I need," you show that you are taking responsibility for your emotions and stating your needs clearly. This invites the other person to respond rather than become defensive.

---

**5. Avoiding Traps and Bad Habits**

Certain speaking habits can inflame conflict rather than resolve it:

1. **Name-Calling**: Insulting the other person's character ("You're lazy" or "You're stupid") can cause them to shut down or shout back.
2. **Broad Accusations**: Words like "always" or "never" are rarely accurate and can make the other person feel attacked.

3. **Threats**: Saying "I'll make you regret this" or similar threats sparks fear and anger, making resolution much harder.
4. **Dragging Up Old Issues**: If the argument is about a current problem, do not bring up every past mistake the other person has made. That will overwhelm them and derail the discussion.
5. **Talking Over**: If both of you talk at once, neither can fully share. It also shows a lack of respect for their turn to speak.

By avoiding these traps, you keep the conversation more focused and fair.

---

## 6. Balancing Logic and Emotion

In a conflict, people have logical points and emotional points. Logical points might include facts, timelines, or evidence ("We agreed on 4 PM; it's written in the text message"). Emotional points might include feelings of disappointment, fear, or anger. Effective speaking balances both. If you ignore emotion, you may sound uncaring. If you ignore logic, you may sound unreasonable. A balanced approach could be: "I know you were busy and that the text said 4 PM. When you came at 5 PM, it made me feel unimportant. I was counting on you to be there earlier."

---

## 7. Tone and Nonverbal Communication

Words are only one part of speaking. Your tone of voice and body language send messages too. A calm tone can help the other person listen, while a sarcastic or yelling tone can make them defensive. Similarly, pointing your finger at them or rolling your eyes can feel like an attack. To speak effectively:

- **Use a Steady Volume**: Not too loud, not too soft.
- **Watch Your Facial Expressions**: A neutral or gentle expression can invite cooperation, while glaring may prompt anger.
- **Avoid Threatening Gestures**: Crossing your arms tightly or shaking a fist is likely to be seen as hostile.

Try practicing your tone and posture in calmer moments, so you know how to manage them during real conflicts.

---

## 8. Structuring Your Message

A clear structure can prevent confusion and ensure your point is made. One method is the "S-F-S-F" approach, which stands for Situation–Feeling–Solution–Future:

1. **Situation**: Describe what happened. Example: "Yesterday evening, I noticed you took my headphones from my desk."
2. **Feeling**: Say how it made you feel. Example: "I felt a bit upset and worried because those are important to me."
3. **Solution**: Suggest or invite a way to fix the problem. Example: "Could you ask me before you borrow them?"
4. **Future**: Say what you hope will happen next time. Example: "That way, I won't be surprised if they're not there, and I'll feel more comfortable letting you use them."

This straightforward pattern helps you keep the conversation on track.

---

## 9. Being Honest Without Being Hurtful

It is essential to share genuine feelings in a conflict, or else the true problem remains hidden. However, honesty should not be confused with harshness. You can be honest while still being thoughtful about your words. For example, instead of saying, "You're completely clueless," you might say, "I don't think you understand my point yet. May I clarify?" This approach keeps your honesty intact but avoids shaming the other person.

If you must point out a mistake or behavior that hurt you, focus on the action, not the person's entire character. "It hurt my feelings when you talked over me in the meeting," is more precise and less hostile than, "You're a rude coworker." Being specific is both honest and fair.

---

## 10. Handling Strong Emotions While Speaking

Sometimes, our feelings in a conflict are overwhelming. We might want to cry, yell, or storm out. Speaking skillfully at these moments takes effort:

- **Pause Before Talking**: If your emotions are very strong, take a moment to calm yourself. Do a few slow breaths or count to ten.

- **Admit Your Feelings**: It is not weak to say, "I'm feeling really angry right now." That can help the other person understand why your voice is shaky or your face is red.
- **Stay on Topic**: Even if you feel the urge to bring up other issues, keep your words focused on the main conflict.
- **Avoid Rushed Words**: Speak more slowly if you can, giving yourself a chance to think about each sentence.
- **Agree to a Break if Needed**: If you sense you are about to say something regrettable, suggest stepping away briefly. This can prevent further harm.

Over time, managing strong emotions while speaking can become easier. Practice helps you stay steady even when you are upset.

---

**11. Encouraging Dialogue**

Conflict resolution works best when both parties speak in turn. A big part of speaking well is also allowing space for the other person to respond. You can encourage them to share by:

- **Inviting Their Thoughts**: "I've shared how I feel. How do you see it?"
- **Asking for Their Ideas**: "What do you think could fix this issue?"
- **Showing You Value Their Input**: "Your opinion is important to me. I'd like to hear your side."

When you speak in a way that welcomes the other person's voice, you are more likely to reach an agreement or at least reduce tension. It shows that you do not just want to talk; you want to solve the conflict together.

---

**12. Examples of Effective Speaking in Conflicts**

Let us look at a couple of short scenarios to see how careful speaking can help:

- **Scenario A**: You and your friend disagree about which movie to watch.
    - **Ineffective**: "You're so stubborn. You never care about what I like!"
    - **Effective**: "I'm disappointed because I was looking forward to seeing this comedy. I feel like I don't get to pick often. Could we talk about choosing a movie that includes some fun elements from both our interests?"

Here, the speaker shares their own feelings, avoids blaming words like "never," and suggests a path forward.

- **Scenario B**: A coworker keeps leaving dirty dishes in the office sink.
  - **Ineffective**: "You're lazy for not washing your cups! Do you think we're your servants?"
  - **Effective**: "I noticed you often leave dishes in the sink. It's starting to bother me because it's extra work for others. Can we agree on a quick rinse policy so the sink stays clean?"

The second version states the facts, expresses concern, and proposes a solution.

---

### 13. Overcoming the Fear of Speaking Up
Some people hesitate to speak in conflicts because they fear anger, rejection, or embarrassment. Overcoming this fear involves a few steps:

1. **Know Your Goal**: Remind yourself why you need to speak. Maybe you want fairness or a clear boundary.
2. **Practice in Low-Stress Settings**: Try expressing minor concerns with people you trust, so you get used to speaking up.
3. **Prepare Your Words**: If you know a conflict is likely, rehearse a few sentences in your mind or on paper.
4. **Use Support**: In bigger conflicts, you might ask a neutral friend or a counselor to be present.
5. **Accept Imperfection**: Speaking up can feel awkward at first. You might stumble over words. This is normal. Each attempt helps you improve.

When you push past the initial fear, you gain confidence. Others may also respect you for honestly sharing your viewpoint rather than staying silent.

---

### 14. Handling Interruptions or Disrespect
Even if you speak skillfully, the other person might interrupt or respond rudely. This can be upsetting. You can handle interruptions or disrespect in a calm way:

- **Stay Polite**: "I'd like to finish what I'm saying, please."

- **Acknowledge Their Urgency**: "I see you have something important to say, but can we keep it in order so we both get a chance to talk fully?"
- **Suggest a Simple Rule**: "How about we each speak for one minute, then switch?"
- **Keep Control of Yourself**: Do not respond to rudeness with more rudeness. You might say, "I understand you're upset, but I'd appreciate if we keep name-calling out of this."

If interruptions persist, you can propose taking a break until both sides agree to more respectful ground rules.

---

## 15. Group Speaking
Speaking in front of a group can be daunting, especially if the group is divided by conflict. To speak effectively:

1. **Plan Key Points**: Write them down if needed, so you do not forget under stress.
2. **Address the Group, but Stay Calm**: Make eye contact around the room. Keep your voice steady.
3. **Stay Brief and Focused**: Long speeches might lose the attention of the group.
4. **Welcome Questions**: Let others know they can ask for more details. This shows you are open to dialogue.
5. **Respect Others' Time**: Do not hog the floor; allow others a turn.
6. **Stay Neutral if You Are the Facilitator**: If you are leading the discussion, focus on fairness, not pushing your own opinion too strongly.

Group speaking often requires you to handle multiple viewpoints at once. Staying centered helps you remain clear and respectful.

---

## 16. Digital Communication
Conflicts can happen over texts, emails, or social media. Written words can be misunderstood because the other person cannot hear your tone or see your face. Here are tips for better digital speaking:

- **Read Twice Before Sending**: Check if your words sound harsher or more critical than you intend.
- **Use Clear Language**: Avoid too many short forms or sarcasm that might confuse the other person.
- **Control Your Pace**: If you are upset, wait a bit before replying. Let yourself cool down.
- **Suggest a Voice Call**: Sometimes, a quick call or video chat can solve misunderstandings faster than back-and-forth messaging.
- **Stay Polite**: Just like face-to-face speaking, avoid insults, threats, or repeated blame.

Keeping digital communication respectful can stop conflicts from growing. If it gets too heated online, propose taking the discussion offline where you can speak more openly and hear each other's tone.

---

**17. Apologizing When Necessary**

Sometimes, we are the ones who spoke harshly or caused hurt. Knowing how to speak an apology is part of good conflict management. A genuine apology includes:

1. **Admitting Fault**: "I said something rude, and that was wrong."
2. **Stating Regret**: "I'm sorry for the words I used. I know they were hurtful."
3. **Mentioning the Impact**: "I realize it made you feel disrespected."
4. **Saying What You'll Do Differently**: "Next time, I'll take a moment to calm down before I speak."
5. **Avoiding Excuses**: "I'm sorry, but I was stressed" can reduce the sincerity. A simple apology is more honest.

A clear apology can help repair trust. It shows you understand your actions had a real effect on the other person, and you plan to change your behavior.

---

**18. Supporting Others Who Struggle to Speak**

Not everyone is comfortable speaking in a conflict. They may be shy or scared. You can help by:

- **Inviting Them Gently**: "Would you like to share what you think?"

- **Giving Them Time**: Do not rush them. Let them gather their thoughts.
- **Expressing Appreciation**: "Thank you for telling me how you feel. That was helpful."
- **Offering to Switch Formats**: If they freeze up in person, let them write their thoughts down or send a short message.

In group settings, you might suggest that each person writes their main points on paper first, then reads them. This can reduce the pressure for those who find speaking aloud difficult.

---

## 19. Long-Term Speaking Growth

Improving speaking skills is not a one-time event. It is an ongoing effort. Consider these steps for long-term growth:

- **Reflect on Past Conversations**: Think about a recent conflict and how you spoke. What worked? What did not?
- **Seek Feedback**: Ask a trusted friend or family member to give honest opinions about your communication style.
- **Study Good Speakers**: Notice how skilled teachers or leaders talk during tough discussions. What do they do that keeps things calm and clear?
- **Practice Self-Control**: When you feel emotions building, practice strategies like breathing or counting to stay calm. This helps you choose your words better.
- **Keep Learning**: Read about conflict resolution or join a club like a debate team if that is available. Trying different communication exercises can sharpen your skills further.

Over time, you will likely see that good speaking habits make conflicts shorter and less stressful, and they often lead to more positive outcomes.

---

## 20. Bringing It All Together

Speaking well in conflict involves more than saying what is on your mind. It means thinking carefully about how your words and tone will be received, making sure you express both logic and emotion, and staying aware of the other person's perspective. It also means knowing when to pause, when to apologize, and how to keep calm in the face of provocation. These skills can transform heated arguments into productive talks.

A short checklist might look like this:

1. **Stay Calm**: Breathe and speak at a measured pace.
2. **Use Respectful Language**: No insults, name-calling, or sweeping accusations.
3. **Be Specific**: Focus on the current issue rather than bringing in past grudges.
4. **Invite Dialogue**: Ask the other person for their view and genuinely listen to it.
5. **Offer or Request Solutions**: Suggest ways forward rather than just complaining.
6. **Apologize When Wrong**: A sincere apology can mend a lot of damage.
7. **Stay Open to Compromise**: If the other person also speaks respectfully, try to meet in the middle.

When we speak in this manner, we reduce the chance of making conflicts worse. Even if the disagreement remains, at least both sides have a clear understanding of each other's thoughts. This is a huge step toward finding common ground or agreeing to a fair plan. Over time, consistent practice of good speaking skills can make us more confident and more effective at handling all kinds of disagreements—whether at home, with friends, at school, or in the workplace.

# Chapter 7: Finding Common Ground

Conflict often involves people who appear to have opposite goals or desires. Yet many times, these opposing sides share at least a few interests. Discovering these shared interests is called finding common ground. When two or more people identify what they agree on, they have a starting point for a better conversation. This starting point can guide them away from blame and anger toward cooperative thinking.

In this chapter, we will look at ways to find common ground in conflicts of different sizes. We will also explore why this step is so important and how it can turn a tense standoff into a calmer interaction. Finding common ground is not about giving in to everything the other person wants. Instead, it is about spotting the places where your goals and their goals overlap. Sometimes, just realizing there is shared ground can lower strong emotions and open the door to real solutions.

---

## 1. The Importance of Shared Interests

To see why common ground matters, let us consider an example. Imagine two friends, Mia and Devin, who cannot agree on how to spend their free weekend. Mia wants to play a video game at home, while Devin wants to go outside and ride bikes. On the surface, it looks like one wants to stay indoors while the other wants to be outdoors. However, they might share an interest in spending time together or having fun. If they can agree that "fun" and "togetherness" are their main goals, they can look for activities that match both. That might mean trying a new game that includes a little exercise outdoors, or splitting their time between a short bike ride and some gaming later.

In more serious conflicts, identifying shared interests is just as powerful. Two classmates might argue about who should present a project, but both want the class to do well. Two people might fight over how to run a club, but both hope the club succeeds. When these deeper common interests become clear—like wanting the best result or caring about the group—they can serve as a steady base for problem-solving.

---

## 2. Shifting from Positions to Interests

A common barrier to finding common ground is that each person focuses on their "position." A position is what someone says they want. For example, "I want the window closed" is a position. "I want the window open" is another position. When people only argue positions, they get stuck. They see no middle path between closed and open.

However, beneath each position often lies an interest. An interest explains why someone wants that position. In the window example, the person who wants the window closed might say, "I feel cold," while the person who wants it open might say, "I feel hot and need fresh air." If both people share the deeper interest of being comfortable, they can think of many ways to meet it. Perhaps they can open the window halfway or use a fan on one side of the room.

Looking for interests instead of positions is a big part of finding common ground. It focuses on reasons rather than just statements. People with seemingly opposite positions might discover that they share bigger interests, like comfort, safety, fairness, or friendship.

---

## 3. Asking the Right Questions

To uncover shared interests, you can ask questions that go deeper than surface positions:

1. **"What do you hope will happen if we go with your idea?"**
   This question reveals what the person actually needs. Maybe they want respect, excitement, or to avoid worry.
2. **"Why is this so important to you?"**
   This invites them to talk about the concerns or values behind their stance.
3. **"If we solve this problem, what would it look like for you?"**
   Their answer might highlight the overall outcome they desire, such as peace or success.
4. **"What do we both agree on here?"**
   Sometimes, people skip this step because they assume there is no agreement. Directly asking can bring to light hidden similarities.

By posing these questions, you shift the conversation from "I want X" or "You must do Y" to "We both want something that could match in some ways." That is the stepping stone to exploring overlap.

## 4. Identifying Shared Values and Goals

Shared values and goals often unite people more than they realize. Two siblings might fight about chores, yet they both value a clean home. Two coworkers might clash over how to approach a project, yet both aim to impress their boss with good work. Parents and teens might argue about curfew, yet both care about safety and personal growth.

To spot shared values or goals, look for the bigger picture. For instance:

- **If the conflict is about chores**: Maybe both siblings value fairness or a neat space.
- **If the conflict is about schedules**: Both parties might care about efficiency or free time.
- **If the conflict is about money**: Both sides might want financial stability or fairness in spending.

When you find a shared goal, say it out loud. For example, "We both want a calm household, so let's figure out a fair way to split chores." Simply stating a shared goal can ease tension, showing that you are not total opposites.

## 5. Examples of Finding Common Ground in Everyday Life

Let us consider a few short scenarios:

**Scenario A: Dispute Over Music Volume**

- **Position A**: "Keep your music down; it is way too loud!"
- **Position B**: "I want to blast my favorite songs!"
- **Deeper Interests**: Person A might need a quiet space to study. Person B might need to relax and feel cheerful. They share the interest of living together peacefully without harming each other's needs. They might

agree that certain times of day should be quieter and other times can be louder if Person A does not have to focus.

**Scenario B: Class Project Decisions**

- **Position A**: "Let's make a poster!"
- **Position B**: "We should do a digital slideshow!"
- **Shared Interest**: Achieving a good grade and impressing the teacher. They can brainstorm ways to use both ideas, such as creating a digital part for the teacher to see on a screen and a smaller poster for the class to view.

**Scenario C: Parent–Child Conflict**

- **Position A** (Parent): "You must be in bed by 9 PM!"
- **Position B** (Child): "I want to stay up until 11 PM!"
- **Shared Interests**: The parent wants the child to be rested and healthy. The child wants some free time in the evening. Both care about the child's well-being. They might work out a compromise where the child goes to bed at a slightly later time than 9 PM, but still early enough to get enough sleep.

In each case, the conflict is less scary once the people involved see they have something in common. Even if the final agreement is not perfect for everyone, just knowing there is a shared goal can set a kinder tone.

---

## 6. The Process of Brainstorming Shared Solutions

Once you identify a shared interest, the next step is generating ideas that fit both sides. Brainstorming means thinking of as many possible ideas as you can, without judging them right away. Later, you narrow down which ideas are realistic. This step often goes hand in hand with finding common ground, because you need a shared direction to guide your brainstorming.

For example, if two siblings both want more free time for fun activities, they might brainstorm ways to do chores faster or in a way that feels more balanced. Maybe they do chores together while listening to music, making it less dull. Perhaps they take turns weekly with certain tasks, so each gets a fair break. By focusing on their shared interest—free time—they can come up with creative ways to reach that goal.

## 7. Working Through Obstacles

Sometimes, even after you find common ground, there are still obstacles. One obstacle might be distrust: you may share an interest, but you do not fully trust the other person to follow through. Another obstacle might be unequal power: one person in the conflict could have more authority or resources. Even so, finding common ground can still help.

- **Distrust**: Build small steps where each person shows good faith. For instance, if you both want a cleaner shared space, you might start by doing small tasks together to prove you can cooperate.
- **Unequal Power**: If someone has more power, it might be harder for the other person to voice their needs. In this case, it can help to call on a neutral adult or authority figure to oversee fairness. But identifying shared interests is still useful. It shows that both sides can benefit from a peaceful outcome.

## 8. The Role of Empathy

Empathy means trying to understand what the other person feels or experiences. Without empathy, finding common ground might feel fake—like you are just looking for a quick fix. With empathy, you genuinely care about whether the other side's needs are met. You do not have to agree with everything the other person says, but you can see why they feel or think a certain way.

Here is how empathy ties in:

1. **Listen for Underlying Concerns**: Ask questions to get the whole picture of why the other person is upset.
2. **Validate Their Feelings**: You can say, "I get why you would be upset about this," even if you see things differently.
3. **Look for a Human Need**: Often, the person wants to feel respected, safe, or valued. Let them know you understand that.

4. **Connect Their Need to Yours**: Show that you also want to be respected, safe, or valued. Now you both see you share a bigger concern.

This approach makes finding common ground more authentic. It also can calm the situation, as most people feel better when they believe their feelings matter.

---

## 9. Common Ground with More Than Two People

Sometimes, a conflict involves three or more people. Maybe it is a group of classmates or family members arguing about how to handle a problem. Finding common ground in a group can be trickier, but the basic idea stays the same: look for anything everyone cares about. For example:

- A club with many members might argue about how to spend club funds. One side wants to buy supplies for a fun event, another side wants educational materials, and another side wants to donate to a cause. If they dig deeper, they might find that they all want the club to have a good reputation and to feel purposeful. This shared interest can guide them to split funds in a way that supports fun, learning, and community support.
- A family might argue about planning a trip. Some want adventure, others want relaxation, and others want to visit relatives. If they realize that the biggest interest is "time spent together," they could plan a trip that includes small amounts of each type of activity.

In groups, it helps to have a person who can guide the discussion by asking everyone what they want most. Then you look for the overlap. It takes patience, but it can lead to better cooperation.

---

## 10. Hidden Agreements

In many conflicts, people focus so much on what they do not have in common that they miss hidden points of agreement. For example, two classmates might argue fiercely about who should do which part of a project. Underneath, maybe they actually agree on wanting the project to be the best in class. They also might agree on deadlines or presentation style. By listing out everything they

60

already see the same way, they can calm down enough to handle the smaller points they still disagree on.

One way to uncover hidden agreements is to write them down. You might say, "Let's write all the things we share or do not argue about." Once you have a list, you can see that not everything is a source of conflict. Sometimes that simple act lowers stress, because the problem feels smaller and more solvable.

## 11. Showing Respect for Differences

Finding common ground does not mean ignoring differences or forcing everyone to think the same. In fact, you can respect the differences while still focusing on what you share. Sometimes, acknowledging that you both see the world differently can actually strengthen cooperation. For instance, two people from different cultures might value traditions that are quite dissimilar, but they can still recognize they both value strong family ties or community harmony.

When you show respect for what makes the other side unique, they are more likely to open up. They feel safer expressing their true concerns, which then helps you both identify the deeper interests you have in common.

## 12. Real-Life Example: Class Committee Argument

Let us imagine a real-life scenario in detail:

A school's student council is planning a community event. Some members want to focus on sports activities, while others want a talent show. The two sides argue for days, each thinking their idea is better. The argument escalates, and soon they cannot agree on anything.

A wise teacher sits them down and asks them to list their shared goals. They find that both sides want:

1. To increase student participation.
2. To raise funds for a local charity.
3. To help students have fun.

Once they see these three shared goals, it becomes easier to brainstorm. They realize they can host a day-long event that starts with sports activities in the morning and ends with a talent show in the afternoon or evening. This plan meets the shared goals of big participation, fundraising, and fun. The two sides do not have to battle for one single idea anymore. They have combined them, all because they found the interests they agreed on.

## 13. Communicating Shared Interests Clearly

After you discover shared ground, you need to communicate it. You can use statements like:

- "We both care about doing this in the best way for everyone, right?"
- "It seems we both want to feel safe and respected."
- "It looks like we agree that the final outcome should be good for both parties."

Announcing these agreements helps everyone refocus. It reminds them that no matter how heated the argument became, they are not enemies in every way. This attitude shift can be enough to prevent further shouting or blaming.

## 14. When Common Ground Seems Hard to Find

Sometimes, you might try to identify shared interests, but the other side insists there are none. They might say, "We have nothing in common. I just want what I want." This can be discouraging, but there are still steps you can try:

1. **Stay Calm and Patient**: Do not force them to admit to common ground right away.
2. **Offer Observations**: "I noticed we both seem upset when we feel ignored. That might be something we share."
3. **Check for Basic Needs**: Even if you disagree on details, you might both need respect, safety, or fairness.
4. **Suggest a Small Starting Point**: "Can we at least agree that we want a solution where nobody feels taken advantage of?" If they agree, that is a small patch of common ground.

It might take time for the other person to see these similarities if they are very upset. Keep the door open and avoid mocking them for not seeing it right away.

## 15. Building Trust Through Shared Efforts

Finding common ground is one thing; acting on it builds trust. If you both discover that you want a respectful friendship, for example, you can make a small plan to show respect daily—like using kind greetings or refraining from mocking. As you follow through with these small actions, the other side sees you are serious. Over time, these acts of good faith can help you work together on bigger problems.

When people take these steps, they change the conflict from "you vs. me" to "us vs. the problem." That is a big shift. It means you are working side by side, looking at the issue as something to solve together. This is often the real key to long-term peace in a conflict.

## 16. Handling Stubbornness

Some conflicts are tough because at least one person is very stubborn. They might keep saying, "My way or no way!" Yet even stubborn people have underlying needs that might match yours. The approach might be slower, but the concept remains:

- **Stay Curious**: Ask questions about what they truly want and why.
- **Speak About Your Own Needs Too**: Be open about what is important to you, so they see they are not the only one who has concerns.
- **Offer Proof of Shared Benefits**: Show how a possible solution meets their needs as well as yours.
- **Avoid Blaming**: Focus on solutions, not on telling them how stubborn they are.

While not every stubborn person will respond immediately, sometimes consistent calmness and a focus on shared interests can chip away at their rigid stance.

## 17. Recognizing When You Do Not Share Goals

In rare cases, you might discover that you and the other side truly have no compatible interests. For example, if someone's interest is to cause harm or to gain complete power, and yours is safety or fairness, you cannot blend those. In such extreme situations, standard conflict resolution methods might not work because the core goals clash completely. Then you might need to seek help from authorities or protect yourself in other ways.

However, these extreme cases are not the norm. In most everyday conflicts—whether at school, at home, or among friends—there is usually at least one area of shared ground, even if it is as simple as both sides wanting to avoid more stress.

## 18. Practical Tips for Finding Common Ground

Below are some practical steps to remember:

1. **Set Aside Blame**: Before you try finding common ground, decide to stop blaming each other for a moment. Blame can block you from seeing any shared point.
2. **Use Friendly Language**: Say things like, "Let's see what we can agree on," or, "Where do we see things the same way?"
3. **Look for Universal Needs**: Often, both sides want to be respected, to feel safe, or to be heard.
4. **Write Down What You Share**: Putting it in writing makes it clearer and reduces confusion.
5. **Brainstorm Around Shared Interests**: After you have named the shared interest (like "We want to keep this friendship strong"), see how many ideas you can gather to protect that interest.
6. **Stay Realistic**: Some shared ground might not solve the entire conflict, but it can reduce it or help you move forward one step at a time.

## 19. Building a Habit of Finding Common Ground

Like any skill, finding common ground becomes easier with practice. You can start by applying it to small disagreements. For instance, if a friend wants to eat at a place you dislike, look for a shared interest: maybe you both want a quick meal, or you both want something healthy. Then find a spot that fits both.

As you practice, you will develop a habit of looking for similarities first rather than diving straight into arguments. This can help prevent conflicts from spiraling out of control. Over time, you might also notice that people start to trust you more because they see you are someone who aims for cooperative solutions.

# Chapter 8: Problem-Solving Steps

When conflict arises, it can feel overwhelming and stressful. People might argue, feel hurt, or shut down completely. One way to handle conflict in a clear, structured way is to follow a set of problem-solving steps. These steps provide a path that takes you from a heated disagreement to a workable solution. By moving through each stage carefully, you avoid jumping to conclusions or letting emotions run the entire show.

In this chapter, we will discuss a practical series of steps you can use to address conflicts of all kinds—from small everyday disagreements to bigger issues that need time and patience. While each conflict is unique, having a steady approach helps ensure you do not miss important details, and it also helps keep the discussion on track.

---

## 1. Define the Problem Clearly

The first step in solving any conflict is to identify what the actual problem is. Sometimes, people argue about a small detail but ignore a deeper cause. Or they might be using vague words like "You are unfair!" without explaining the specific action that upset them. To avoid confusion:

- **Be Specific**: If two siblings argue about "not being fair with chores," define precisely which chores are at issue and who is doing what.
- **Focus on One Issue at a Time**: If the problem is that your friend always cancels plans, talk about that first rather than bringing in extra complaints.
- **Check for Agreement on the Definition**: Ask, "Do we both see this as the main problem?" If the other person disagrees on what the conflict is about, you need to clarify further.

By clearly stating the problem, you make sure both sides are addressing the same thing. This prevents misunderstandings later.

## 2. Gather Information and Perspectives

Once you agree on the problem, gather more details. This includes each person's viewpoint, the facts of the situation, and any relevant background. For example, if the conflict is about a school project, gather details like the project requirements, who was assigned to do what, and any deadlines. If the conflict involves family rules, understand what those rules are and why they were set.

- **Ask Open-Ended Questions**: "How do you see this situation?" "What led you to believe this was unfair?"
- **Consider Feelings**: Both facts and emotions matter. If your sibling feels overlooked, that feeling is part of the conflict.
- **Avoid Quick Judgments**: Listen calmly, and remember that the other side's perspective may differ from yours, even if you have the same facts.
- **Take Notes if Needed**: Writing down key points can help when you are trying to remember details, especially in bigger conflicts or group settings.

This step helps everyone get a complete picture before moving on to solutions. If you skip it, you might come up with ideas that do not really address the actual situation.

---

## 3. Identify Interests and Goals

You have already defined the problem and gathered information. Now it is time to see why each person cares about the issue. Each side likely has interests they want to protect. Recall from the previous chapter how identifying common ground can help. Here, you list out both the shared and separate interests.

- **List Separate Interests**: For instance, one person might value quiet time, while the other values freedom to play music.
- **List Shared Interests**: Perhaps both sides value respect in the shared living space.
- **Remember Feelings**: If someone feels disrespected or worried, that is an interest too.

Doing this step ensures that when you look for solutions, you try to meet as many of these interests as possible. When people feel their needs are noticed, they are less likely to keep arguing.

## 4. Brainstorm Possible Solutions

Now comes a creative part: brainstorming. In this step, you generate as many ideas as you can to solve the defined problem. The rule is: do not judge any ideas yet. Just list them. This encourages creativity and helps you see options you might miss if you filter them too soon.

1. **Set a Brainstorm Time**: For a few minutes, each person can say or write down ideas.
2. **No Criticism Yet**: Even if an idea sounds silly, keep it on the list.
3. **Encourage Wild Thoughts**: Sometimes a playful suggestion leads to a good variation.
4. **Combine Ideas**: If one person suggests sharing resources, and another suggests a schedule, see if both can be merged.

When brainstorming in a group, it can help to go around in a circle. Each person offers one idea at a time. This ensures no single person dominates the process. The main aim is to find a range of potential solutions that address the interests you listed in the previous step.

## 5. Evaluate the Ideas

Once you have a list of possible solutions, move to the next step: evaluation. Now you look at each idea and discuss whether it meets the different interests involved. You might ask:

- Does it respect both sides' feelings?
- Is it fair in terms of workload, cost, or time?
- Is it realistic with the resources we have?
- Would both parties actually follow through?
- Does it harm anyone or break any rules?

During this evaluation, you should also consider the pros and cons of each idea. For example, if one idea is easy to do but does not fix the main issue, that might not be the best choice. Another idea might solve the main issue but requires a lot of time or money, which might or might not be acceptable to everyone.

## 6. Choose the Best Solution or Solutions

After evaluating the ideas, choose the option (or combination of options) that best meets the interests of all sides. Sometimes, you might pick more than one approach, especially if there are multiple parts to the conflict. Other times, you might need a compromise, where each side gives up something and gains something else.

It is important that both parties agree on the choice. If one side feels forced, they might not carry it out later. This is why mutual agreement matters in conflict resolution. You might ask, "Can we both live with this solution?" or "Do we both feel okay about trying this idea?"

---

## 7. Create an Action Plan

A solution without a clear action plan can remain just an idea. In this step, you specify who will do what, by when, and how you will check on progress. For example:

- **Who**: Which person is responsible for each task?
- **What**: What exactly will they do?
- **When**: What is the timeline or deadline for each step?
- **Resources**: Do you need any items or help to make it happen?
- **Review**: How will you know if the plan is working?

A well-defined plan might look like this: "Sam will clean the shared living area on Mondays, and Alex will do it on Thursdays. They will each spend 30 minutes sweeping, wiping surfaces, and tidying up. We will check in every Sunday night to see if we want to adjust the tasks."

By being specific, you reduce the chance for future confusion. Everyone knows what is expected.

---

## 8. Implement and Observe

Next, you carry out the plan. This might be the most challenging part because people can slip back into old habits or forget to do their tasks. It is helpful to keep track:

- **Follow the Plan**: Do your assigned tasks as you agreed.
- **Stay Aware of Changes**: If something unexpected happens—like a new schedule or a sudden problem—note it and see if the plan needs revisiting.
- **Encourage Each Other**: If it is a shared plan, small positive comments like "Thanks for doing your part" can keep everyone motivated.

---

## 9. Review and Adjust if Needed

Even the best solution can need tweaking. That is why you review the outcome after some time. Ask questions like:

- **Is the conflict mostly resolved?**
- **Are we both happier with this approach than before?**
- **Is there anything we did not address that is still bothering someone?**
- **Do we need a slight change to make it more fair or simpler?**

If something is not working, go back a step or two. Maybe you need to brainstorm again or choose a different idea. This does not mean the conflict cannot be solved; it just means the first solution was not a perfect fit. Making small adjustments can often fix issues and keep the peace.

---

## 10. Example of the Problem-Solving Steps in Action

Imagine two classmates, Jenna and Luis, who share a desk at school. They keep arguing about who sits on which side, leading to them shoving each other's stuff around.

1. **Define the Problem**
   They define the problem as: "We can't agree on how to share our desk space properly."
2. **Gather Information**
   - Jenna says she feels cramped because Luis's papers spill over.
   - Luis says he has large books that do not fit well, and Jenna moves his items aside.

- Both get annoyed when their materials are touched without permission.

3. **Identify Interests and Goals**
    - Jenna wants enough room for her notebooks and does not want to keep pushing things around.
    - Luis wants space for his big books and does not want Jenna to move his stuff.
    - They share an interest in a calm classroom and not getting in trouble for arguing.

4. **Brainstorm Solutions**
    - Put a line of tape down the middle of the desk.
    - Have a rotating schedule, where one day Jenna uses more space, the next day Luis does.
    - Ask the teacher for a second small table for extra books.
    - Use vertical space by stacking books in a small stand.
    - Switch seats with other students who might need less desk space.

5. **Evaluate Ideas**
    - Tape down the middle: simple to do, but does not solve big books taking too much room.
    - Rotating schedule: might cause confusion on who gets more space when.
    - Extra small table: depends on whether the teacher can provide one.
    - Using a small stand: this seems practical and cheap if the teacher allows it.
    - Switching seats: might cause new conflicts if the new seat buddy also needs space.

6. **Choose the Best Option**
    They decide to try a two-part approach:
    - Ask for a small stand to hold Luis's larger books on top or next to the desk.
    - Place a thin strip of tape to mark a fair division, but with enough space for both.

7. **Create an Action Plan**
    - Luis will speak to the teacher after class about the stand.
    - Jenna will put the tape on the desk at a time the teacher allows.
    - They agree to each keep their items within their marked section once it is done.

8. **Implement and Observe**
   - Over the next week, they follow this plan. The teacher gives them a small stand for books. Jenna places the tape, and they both keep their materials in their own section.
9. **Review and Adjust**
   - After a week, they check in. Jenna is happier because she has her own clear space. Luis is glad his books are not squashed. They decide everything is working fine. No adjustment is needed.

By following the steps, they solved a small but annoying conflict. Neither had to "win" while the other "lost." Instead, each got part of what they needed, and the classroom stayed calmer.

---

## 11. Handling Bigger or Ongoing Conflicts

Some conflicts are not as simple as a shared desk. They might be about long-standing issues within a family or friend group. In such cases, the same steps still apply, but you might need more time:

- **Longer Discussions**: You might have to repeat the "gather information" step multiple times to uncover all concerns.
- **Deeper Emotions**: Strong feelings can slow the process. You may need breaks to manage anger or sadness.
- **Possible Outside Help**: A counselor, teacher, or mediator can guide you if the conflict is too complex.
- **Written Agreements**: In bigger conflicts, it can help to write down the final plan so nobody forgets.

Staying patient and respectful is key. Even if it takes multiple meetings, following a clear problem-solving approach helps prevent the conflict from growing larger.

---

## 12. Group Problem-Solving

When three or more people are involved, you can use the same steps, but you need to be sure every voice is heard. Some tips for group problem-solving:

1. **Assign a Facilitator**: This person makes sure everyone follows the steps and has a chance to speak.
2. **Set Rules for Speaking**: No interruptions, and each person gets equal time.
3. **Use Visual Aids**: Write down the problem, interests, and solutions on a board or large paper.
4. **Encourage Everyone's Input**: Each group member should contribute to brainstorming and evaluation.
5. **Aim for Shared Agreement**: The final plan should feel fair to the majority, if not all, of the group.

Large groups can get messy if people talk over each other or push their own ideas without listening. A structured method helps keep the discussion fair and clear.

---

## 13. Staying Open-Minded

One challenge in problem-solving is being too fixed on your own preferred solution. If you ignore all other ideas, you might miss a path that works for both sides. Being open-minded means:

- **Listening Carefully**: Even if an idea sounds strange at first, consider how it might meet shared interests.
- **Welcoming Adjustments**: Your initial solution might need tweaking. Stay flexible.
- **Accepting Partial Wins**: Sometimes, neither side gets 100% of what they want, but both sides get enough to be comfortable.

This openness helps everyone move from "I must have it all" to "Let's find a solution we can both accept."

---

## 14. Communicating During Each Step

Good communication is vital at every step. If you are talking over others or hiding information, the problem-solving approach stalls. Here are some reminders:

- **Use Simple and Direct Language**: Be clear about what you want to say.
- **Ask Clarifying Questions**: If you do not understand an idea, ask politely for more details.
- **Show Respect**: No mocking or putting down someone's suggestions.
- **Take Turns**: Let each person speak without interruption.
- **Summarize**: Now and then, restate what has been decided so everyone stays on the same page.

When each step is handled with respectful communication, the conflict is less likely to flare up again midway.

---

## 15. Handling Emotional Spikes

During problem-solving, emotions might spike. Maybe someone feels their suggestion was dismissed, or they recall a past hurt. Here is how to manage emotional moments:

- **Pause the Discussion**: If voices rise or tears start, it might be time for a short break.
- **Acknowledge Feelings**: Say something like, "I see you're upset. Let's take a moment to understand what's bothering you."
- **Refocus on the Steps**: Remind everyone, "We are on the brainstorming step right now. We will evaluate your idea soon."
- **Return When Ready**: Only resume once the tension has lowered a bit.

Emotions are natural, but letting them overpower the entire method can derail the process.

---

## 16. Checking for Fairness

Fairness is a big concern in conflict resolution. One side might worry they are giving up too much, or that the other side gets an easier deal. During the evaluation phase, it helps to ask:

- **Does this solution place too much burden on one person?**
- **Does everyone share some of the responsibility or cost?**

- Is there a balance between what each side gives and gets?

If something seems off, adjust the plan. Perhaps each side can trade tasks or split costs in a more balanced way. Fairness does not always mean things are split exactly 50/50, but it does mean both sides feel respected and not cheated.

---

## 17. Following Through

Agreeing on a solution is only half the battle. If people do not follow through, the conflict will come back. You can improve follow-through by:

- **Setting Reminders**: Use notes or phone alerts if the plan involves daily tasks.
- **Having Regular Check-Ins**: Maybe once a week, see if everyone is doing what they promised.
- **Offering Support**: If one side struggles with their part, see if you can help or adjust.
- **Addressing Problems Early**: If something is not working, bring it up right away rather than waiting for it to explode into a new fight.

This helps keep the solution active instead of letting it fade away.

---

## 18. Problem-Solving with Authority Figures

Sometimes, the person you are in conflict with has more power—like a teacher or parent. You can still use these steps, but you might need to adapt:

- **Respect Their Role**: A teacher or parent might have the final say, but you can still present your viewpoint using these steps.
- **Provide Clear Reasons**: Show that you have thought through the problem logically. This can make them more open to listening.
- **Ask for Their Perspective**: Authority figures also have interests, such as student well-being or household safety.
- **Suggest a Trial**: If you want to propose a new rule or approach, ask if you can test it for a short period.

While they might still make the final call, showing you are methodical can influence them to be more flexible.

## 19. The Benefits of a Structured Approach

Why go through all these steps? Because a methodical approach reduces the chance of jumping to unfair conclusions or ignoring someone's real needs. It also provides a roadmap so that even if emotions run high, you can say, "Let's stick to the steps." This can calm people down and remind them that you are working toward a common solution.

Additional benefits include:

- **Less Guessing**: You clearly see what each side wants.
- **Reduced Blame**: The focus is on facts, interests, and solutions rather than pointing fingers.
- **Better Cooperation**: People who feel heard and involved in the process are more likely to honor the outcome.
- **Consistency**: You can apply the same steps to various conflicts, from small arguments to bigger group disputes.

# Chapter 9: Conflict at Home

Home is where people spend a lot of time together, and it can be a cozy place of support. Yet it can also be where arguments happen often. Family members see one another's daily habits, have to share resources, and follow routines. Different personalities, ages, and priorities can all clash under one roof. When conflicts happen at home, they can be stressful because we usually cannot walk away and never see our family again. Instead, we must find ways to live together in peace. This chapter will explore common causes of conflict at home, along with tips and tools for fixing these problems in a caring and respectful way.

---

## 1. Why Conflict at Home Feels Different

Home conflicts might feel more intense than conflicts in other places. Here are some reasons:

1. **Close Relationships**: We care deeply about our family members. An unkind word from a parent or sibling can hurt more than the same comment from a stranger.
2. **Limited Space and Resources**: People in one household share rooms, bathrooms, appliances, and sometimes even devices like computers or game consoles. Sharing can lead to disagreements if there is no fair plan.
3. **Daily Interaction**: We see family members day after day. If a conflict is not resolved, it keeps popping up.
4. **Power Differences**: Adults usually have more authority than children. This can cause tension if a child feels they have no say, or if a parent feels disrespected.
5. **Family History**: In a family, people often remember past arguments. Old hurts can surface during new conflicts, making them bigger.

Because of these factors, conflict at home can easily become heated. People might say things they regret or carry negative feelings for a long time. However, home can also be a place where we learn healthy ways of handling disagreements, improving our relationships in the process.

---

## 2. Common Causes of Conflict at Home

Home conflicts can arise for many reasons. Below are a few frequent triggers:

- **Chores and Responsibilities**: Who cleans the kitchen? Who takes out the trash? Who does the laundry? When someone feels overburdened or believes another person is lazy, tension can build.
- **Personal Space and Privacy**: Siblings might fight about someone entering their room without knocking or borrowing items without asking.
- **Schedules and Routines**: Family members may clash over bedtime, wake-up time, use of the bathroom, or meal times.
- **Money and Budgets**: In some households, parents may argue about spending or saving. Teens might want money for hobbies or clothes. Limited funds can spark arguments if people feel their needs are ignored.
- **Rules and Discipline**: Children might disagree with parents about screen time or curfews. Parents might feel children are not respecting house rules, while children feel those rules are unfair.
- **Differences in Values**: Parents and kids might have different opinions about music, clothing, friends, or lifestyle choices.
- **Sibling Rivalry**: Brothers and sisters might compete for attention or resources. They can argue over fairness, feel jealous, or tease each other in ways that escalate into bigger fights.

These triggers vary from one home to another. Some families have big fights over chores but not about money. Others hardly care about chores but argue about how to spend free time. Recognizing your specific triggers is the first step to stopping arguments before they turn into major battles.

---

## 3. Sibling Conflicts

Siblings often argue because they share so much: parents, space, possessions, and time. A few reasons sibling conflict can arise:

1. **Competition for Attention**: Kids might feel one sibling is the "favorite" or gets more praise, which can lead to arguments or attempts to show who is better.
2. **Differences in Age and Ability**: An older child might think the younger one is too messy or too loud, while the younger child might feel bossed around.

3. **Personality Clashes**: One sibling might enjoy quiet activities, while another loves loud music and social gatherings, causing annoyance.
4. **Unresolved Past Hurts**: If a sibling once broke a favorite toy or made a hurtful comment, the other sibling may carry that anger forward, making new conflicts worse.

How to Handle Sibling Conflicts

- **Set Clear Rules**: Parents can help by creating guidelines about privacy, borrowing items, or noise levels.
- **Encourage Communication**: Ask siblings to talk about what bothers them rather than fighting physically or trading insults.
- **Give Personal Space**: Each sibling might need a corner or a box where they can keep personal items that nobody else touches.
- **Fair Division of Tasks**: Chores and privileges should match each child's age and ability, reducing claims of unfairness.
- **Teach Apologies and Forgiveness**: Siblings can learn to say "I'm sorry" and accept each other's apologies, healing smaller hurt feelings before they become major problems.

---

## 4. Parent-Child Conflicts

Parents usually hold the power in a household, including setting rules and limits. Children, especially teenagers, might push back as they seek more independence. This can lead to conflict over:

- **Curfew and Social Activities**: A teen might want to stay out late with friends, while parents worry about safety.
- **Screen Time**: Parents might limit phone or game use, and children might see it as unfair.
- **Academic Expectations**: Parents may want a child to focus more on homework or get better grades, causing pressure and resentment if the child feels misunderstood.
- **House Rules**: Conflicts can arise if children do not follow rules about cleaning up, respecting bedtime, or limiting junk food.

### Strategies for Parent-Child Conflicts

- **Explain Reasons**: Parents who share the reasoning behind rules (like health or safety) often face less resistance. Children might follow rules more willingly if they understand the purpose.
- **Negotiation and Compromise**: Finding a middle ground—like adjusting a curfew a little later on weekends—can prevent constant battles.
- **Consistent Boundaries**: If rules keep changing or are enforced randomly, it can lead to confusion and more conflict.
- **Active Listening**: Parents should listen to a child's concerns without jumping to punish or dismiss them. Children should also try to understand parents' worries or responsibilities.
- **Positive Reinforcement**: Encouraging good behavior with praise or privileges can sometimes be more effective than scolding or punishment.

---

## 5. Conflict Among Parents or Caregivers

Children notice when the adults in the home argue. Tension between parents or caregivers can create an atmosphere of stress. Common triggers include:

- **Money Issues**: Disagreements over bills, spending habits, or saving.
- **Different Parenting Styles**: One parent might be more strict, while the other is more relaxed.
- **Household Responsibilities**: Each parent might feel the other is not doing a fair share of tasks like cleaning, cooking, or childcare.
- **Work Stress**: Jobs can cause fatigue, leading adults to snap at each other over small things.
- **Lack of Time Together**: Busy schedules might make it hard for adults to communicate well, and misunderstandings can pile up.

When parents fight constantly, children can feel anxious or believe they are at fault. Parents who learn to handle conflict in respectful, calm ways can set a powerful example for their kids.

---

## 6. Communication Tips for Families

Good communication is the heart of conflict resolution at home. Here are some family-focused tips:

1. **Family Meetings**: Setting aside a regular time when everyone can discuss issues helps prevent resentment. Each person gets a turn to speak while others listen.
2. **Use Neutral Language**: Words like "We need to work out a plan" are more inviting than "You always do this wrong."
3. **Avoid Yelling**: Raising your voice can make others defensive or scared. Lower tones often get better responses.
4. **Speak About Feelings**: Saying "I feel upset because…" can help family members understand your perspective.
5. **Suggest Solutions**: Rather than only complaining, offer ideas on how to fix the problem.
6. **Summarize What Others Say**: This shows you listened. For instance, "I hear that you feel overworked. You want us to share chores more evenly."
7. **No Teasing or Mocking**: Even playful-sounding jokes can hurt if someone is sensitive about the topic.

Families that build a habit of talking things out calmly are better able to handle problems before they explode into big fights.

## 7. Specific Strategies for Chore Conflicts

A very common household conflict is chores. Here are simple ways to address this issue:

- **Make a Chore Chart**: List all the tasks that need to be done daily or weekly. Assign a name next to each task. Rotate tasks regularly if fairness is a concern.
- **Agree on Rewards or Consequences**: If chores are done well, perhaps the person earns a small reward (like picking a family movie). If chores are skipped, there is a clear consequence (like losing some privileges).
- **Set Realistic Expectations**: Make sure tasks match a person's age and ability. A six-year-old can help tidy toys, but probably not clean the entire kitchen.
- **Schedule Chore Time**: Pick a specific day or time to do chores together as a family. This can reduce arguments about who is not doing their part.
- **Explain the Why**: Remind everyone that chores keep the home clean and comfortable, benefiting all members.

When chores are managed fairly and clearly, conflicts about who does (or does not do) what can lessen over time.

## 8. Handling Curfew and Rules Conflicts

Children and teens often want more freedom than parents allow. Parents worry about safety, responsibility, or school performance. To handle these fights:

- **Lay Out Expectations**: Parents should clearly state rules and the reasons behind them. For example: "We want you home by 9 PM on weeknights because you need enough rest for school."
- **Listen to the Child's View**: The child might have good reasons for wanting a later curfew, such as a part-time job, a sports practice, or an important event with friends.
- **Negotiate**: If the parent sees the child is responsible, they might extend the curfew slightly. If the child proves they can stick to this new time without issues, maybe it can be extended further.
- **Set Consequences for Breaking Rules**: If a teen stays out too late, discuss a fair consequence ahead of time. Make sure the consequence is known and reasonable.
- **Stay Consistent**: Random exceptions can confuse everyone. Consistency builds trust and respect.

When children see that rules are based on real concerns, and that there is some room for growth, they may become less likely to rebel just for the sake of rebelling.

---

## 9. Addressing Deeper Emotional Conflicts

Not all home conflicts are about chores or curfews. Some are tied to deeper emotional issues:

- **Feeling Unloved or Unheard**: A child might act out because they feel they are never listened to. A parent might lose patience because they feel disrespected.
- **Past Trauma**: If the family went through a big crisis (a move, a job loss, a loss in the family), leftover stress can cause more frequent arguments.
- **Comparisons and Expectations**: A child may feel compared to a sibling who does better academically or in sports, causing resentment.

For these deeper issues, open conversation is crucial. Family counseling can also help if emotions are too tangled to handle alone. Sometimes, having a neutral professional guide the discussion can bring hidden hurts into the light, letting each person feel safe to share and heal.

---

## 10. Balancing Power in the Household

Parents need to guide and protect children, which naturally means they have more authority. But kids, especially as they grow into their teenage years, want to have some say in their lives. Striking a balance can reduce conflicts:

- **Family Decision-Making**: Let children have a voice on certain decisions (like family outings or how to rearrange the living room). This shows respect for their opinions.
- **Clear Boundaries**: Explain which decisions are not negotiable (such as health and safety issues) while leaving some room for choice in other areas.
- **Building Trust**: If a child shows responsibility, parents can offer more freedom. If that freedom is misused, parents can step back until trust is rebuilt.
- **Listening to Parents' Concerns**: Children can also help by understanding that parents worry because they care, not because they want to control them.

A balanced approach can prevent power struggles where each side feels forced to shout or give ultimatums.

---

## 11. When a Family Member Refuses to Cooperate

In some households, one person might refuse to discuss problems or change their behavior. This can be especially hard if that person is a parent or an older sibling who does not want to compromise. What can others do?

1. **Stay Calm and Polite**: Responding with anger might make them dig in further.
2. **Explain the Impact**: Gently share how their behavior affects the rest of the family. "When you leave dishes everywhere, it makes the house messy for everyone."

3. **Seek Support**: Talk to another trusted adult, such as a grandparent, an aunt or uncle, or a counselor, if the problem is severe.
4. **Set Personal Boundaries**: Even if you cannot force them to change, you can decide how you react. For example, if a sibling always yells, you can say, "I won't continue talking if we're yelling. Let's speak when we're calm."
5. **Consider Mediation**: Sometimes a mediator—another adult or professional—can help both sides communicate better.

Change might be slow, but showing consistent patience and respect can slowly encourage the uncooperative person to consider a better approach.

## 12. The Role of Apologies and Forgiveness in the Home

Home conflicts can be frequent. If left unaddressed, they build bitterness over time. Apologies and forgiveness are powerful tools:

- **Apologies**: When you realize you have made a mistake—like yelling or insulting—own up to it. A genuine apology can calm a heated situation.
- **Forgiveness**: Holding grudges at home can poison daily life. If someone shows genuine regret, try to let go of anger.
- **Leading by Example**: Parents who apologize to their children when wrong teach kids that it is okay to admit mistakes.

Forgiveness does not mean forgetting or ignoring harmful actions. It means deciding not to hold onto anger in a way that hurts the entire household. In time, trust can be rebuilt if everyone works on respectful behavior.

## 13. Conflict Over Cultural or Generational Differences

Some families have members from different generations or cultural backgrounds living together. Conflicts can arise if grandparents have more traditional views, parents are somewhere in the middle, and children have modern tastes. Here are ways to handle that:

- **Show Respect for Traditions**: Even if you do not share the same beliefs, try to understand why they matter to older family members.

- **Explain the Present World**: If grandparents do not grasp social media or modern music, calmly explain what they are about and why they are popular.
- **Celebrate Small Agreements**: Find areas where you do see eye to eye—maybe on the importance of kindness or the joy of spending time together.
- **Compromise**: If older relatives want certain customs followed, you can do them respectfully in some cases, while also asking them to accept certain new ways in others.
- **Avoid Mocking**: Laughing at someone else's customs or calling them "old-fashioned" can block healthy dialogue.

When family members bridge generational or cultural gaps through mutual respect, conflicts in that area can often be reduced.

---

## 14. Managing Stress and Emotional Outbursts

At home, people can feel safe enough to show their true emotions—which can be good, but can also lead to big outbursts. Stressed parents might snap at kids, or siblings might have screaming fights. How to handle this?

- **Recognize Stress**: If you had a bad day at school or work, tell your family you need a bit of time before discussing an issue.
- **Set a Cool-Down Period**: Agree that if tempers flare, you will take a break (like 10 minutes of calm) and then return to discuss the problem.
- **Practice Soothing Techniques**: Deep breathing, counting to ten, or taking a short walk can help.
- **Stay Mindful of Triggers**: If you know you explode when you are hungry or tired, address those needs before tackling tough conversations.
- **Support Each Other**: If you see a family member is stressed, offer a kind word or help them with a task, which might prevent an argument from starting.

---

## 15. Technology and Screen Conflicts

Modern households often deal with conflicts over phone, tablet, or computer use:

- **Set Family Tech Guidelines**: Decide as a group what the rules are for screen time on school nights, weekends, and mealtimes.
- **Common Charging Station**: Have a spot where devices go at a certain time each evening, so nobody is sneaking off with a phone late at night.
- **Explain Health Concerns**: Too much screen time can affect sleep or cause eye strain. Understanding this can motivate better habits.
- **Schedule Offline Activities**: Plan some family fun or chores that require everyone to be off their devices.
- **Balance Freedom and Responsibility**: If a teen or child shows they can manage screen time responsibly, they might earn more freedom.

When technology usage is discussed openly and fairly, it can reduce daily arguments over phone and computer privileges.

---

## 16. Family Meetings for Conflict Resolution

A family meeting can be a powerful way to address home conflicts. Here is how to do it:

1. **Set a Regular Time**: Maybe once a week or once a month, gather the household.
2. **Choose a Comfortable Setting**: Sit around a table or in the living room, where everyone can see each other.
3. **Have an Agenda**: Start with positives—what went well that week—then move to problems people want to discuss.
4. **Use Good Communication Habits**: Let each person speak without interruption. Summarize points, ask clarifying questions.
5. **Brainstorm Solutions Together**: If a recurring conflict is chores, discuss how to fix that problem so it feels fair to all.
6. **Write Down Agreements**: If you settle on a plan, note it. This helps avoid confusion later.
7. **End on a Positive Note**: Find a shared good moment or goal to wrap up the meeting.

Regular family meetings can stop small problems from growing larger by ensuring everyone has a chance to speak before resentment builds.

## 17. Dealing with Persistent or Serious Family Conflicts

Some issues run deep and do not go away after a single conversation. If your household faces serious, ongoing problems:

- **Counseling or Therapy**: A family counselor can help people communicate more effectively and deal with underlying issues.
- **Involving a Trusted Relative**: Sometimes, an older cousin, uncle, or grandparent can mediate if they are neutral and respected.
- **Seeking Community Help**: If arguments involve issues like substance abuse, violence, or severe mental health concerns, a professional or community service may be necessary.
- **Safety First**: If anyone feels unsafe or experiences abuse, it is essential to reach out to a trusted adult, teacher, or helpline right away.

Persistent conflicts can be more complex than everyday disagreements. They may require time, patience, and outside support to resolve. That does not mean they cannot improve. With the right help, families can find healthier ways to live together.

---

## 18. Teaching Children Conflict Skills Early

When parents teach kids basic conflict resolution from a young age, it can prevent bigger fights in the future. Examples:

- **Sharing and Taking Turns**: Encouraging kids to wait their turn and share toys fosters respect for others.
- **Using Words Instead of Force**: Teach them to say "I don't like that, please stop" instead of hitting or grabbing.
- **Listening and Repeating**: Show them how to listen to what their sibling or friend said and repeat it to show understanding.
- **Small Agreements**: Even toddlers can learn to make choices ("Do you want the red cup or the blue cup?"), which helps them feel heard.

These lessons may be simple, but they form the base of healthy conflict resolution skills. As kids grow, they build on these habits rather than defaulting to yelling or fighting.

# Chapter 10: Conflict at School

School is a place where students go to learn, but it is also a social environment with many people of different ages, backgrounds, and personalities. This can lead to all sorts of conflicts: from small disagreements between classmates to bigger issues involving teachers, staff, or entire groups. Because you spend so many hours at school each week, an unresolved conflict there can become stressful. However, school can also be a great place to practice conflict resolution skills. This chapter will look at common school conflicts and ways to address them calmly.

## 1. Why Conflicts Arise at School

School conflicts happen for several reasons:

1. **Diverse Personalities**: Each class has students with different ways of thinking, leading to clashes if people do not respect each other's styles.
2. **Peer Pressure**: Teens might tease each other to fit in with a group or act out to look "cool," causing hurt feelings.
3. **Academic Stress**: Homework, tests, and group projects can create tension if people feel overloaded or blamed for poor performance.
4. **Competition**: Some students may compete for top grades, sports positions, or popularity. Competition can spark jealousy or arguments.
5. **Rules and Authority**: Students might not agree with certain school rules, leading to conflict with teachers or administrators.
6. **Gossip and Rumors**: False or exaggerated information can spread quickly, damaging friendships or reputations.

Recognizing these triggers can help students and teachers address problems before they grow into serious conflicts.

## 2. Conflict Between Classmates

Many student-versus-student conflicts begin with small issues:

- **Seating**: Who sits where can matter if some students hog certain desks or save seats for friends, leaving others feeling excluded.
- **Classroom Supplies**: Arguments can start when classmates take pencils, markers, or calculators without asking, or do not return them.
- **Teasing and Name-Calling**: Some students might tease others about clothing, appearance, or interests. Even "light-hearted" teasing can hurt if the other person is sensitive.
- **Group Projects**: Group work can go wrong if one person does not do their share, or if a bossy classmate tries to control the whole project.
- **Jealousy**: Seeing a classmate excel in sports or music can make others jealous, and if this jealousy is not handled calmly, it can turn into bullying or spiteful comments.

**How to Handle Classmate Conflicts**

- **Talk Directly**: If someone is bothering you, calmly let them know. "I felt upset when you took my book without asking."
- **Offer Solutions**: "If you want to share my markers, please ask first, and I'll say yes if I'm not using them."
- **Seek Peer Mediation**: Some schools have trained students or staff to help classmates settle disputes.
- **Walk Away from Provocations**: If a classmate tries to start a fight or teases you to get a reaction, stepping away can stop it from escalating.
- **Tell a Trusted Adult**: If the conflict involves threats, repeated bullying, or physical harm, involve a teacher or counselor.

---

## 3. Conflict with Teachers

Students can have disagreements with teachers over grades, classroom rules, or disciplinary actions. Some possible sources of tension:

- **Grades and Feedback**: A student might believe they deserved a higher grade, while the teacher feels the work was incomplete or below standards.
- **Classroom Behavior**: If a teacher thinks a student is disrespectful or disruptive, they may give warnings or send the student out of class, which the student may find unfair.

- **Miscommunication**: A student might misunderstand a teacher's instructions or expectations, resulting in late or incorrect assignments.
- **Personality Clashes**: Sometimes, a student and a teacher just do not click. Their styles of speaking or thinking clash, leading to tension.

**Ways to Resolve Student-Teacher Conflicts**

- **Speak After Class**: Politely ask for a few minutes to explain your concerns or to understand the teacher's viewpoint in private.
- **Stay Respectful**: Even if you disagree, using a calm voice and polite words can help the teacher stay open to your points.
- **Ask for Specific Feedback**: If you are confused about a grade, request more details on how you can improve next time.
- **Check the Rules**: If a rule or punishment seems unfair, ask where it is stated in the school's policy or class guidelines.
- **Involve a Counselor**: If direct talk fails, ask a counselor or another teacher to mediate. Sometimes a neutral adult can help both sides see each other's view.
- **Suggest a Solution**: If you have a plan to fix a problem—like redoing an assignment or adjusting your behavior in class—offer it. This shows you are serious about solving the issue.

Most teachers want students to succeed. Showing maturity and respect can encourage them to meet you halfway, even if they hold authority in the classroom.

---

## 4. Conflict Over School Rules or Policies

Students might disagree with school rules about uniforms, cell phone use, or tardiness. They may feel some rules are old-fashioned or unfair. However, schools create policies to maintain order and safety. If you think a rule is unreasonable:

1. **Learn the Reason**: Maybe the school prohibits phones to avoid distractions or cheating. Understanding the goal might soften your view.
2. **Find the Right Channel**: Some schools have a student council or suggestion box where you can voice concerns.

3. **Propose Alternatives**: Instead of just complaining, suggest a revised rule. For instance, "Phones can be used at lunchtime but not in class."
4. **Stay Polite and Organized**: If you gather signatures or write a letter to the principal, keep it respectful and solution-focused.
5. **Know When to Accept**: If the school stands by the policy and it does not violate basic rights, you may need to follow it even if you dislike it.

---

## 5. Group Projects and Team Conflicts

Group projects can be a big source of conflict because students have to rely on each other. Here are common issues:

- **Uneven Participation**: One or two group members do most of the work, while others coast along.
- **Different Work Styles**: Some students like to plan early, while others delay. Some want to meet in person, others prefer online chats.
- **Arguments Over Roles**: Conflicts can arise if everyone wants to be the leader or if nobody wants to take responsibility.
- **Deadline Stress**: Last-minute rushes can cause finger-pointing or panic if the project is not finished on time.

**Tips for Smooth Group Work**

- **Set Clear Roles Early**: Decide who will handle research, writing, visuals, and presentations. Write it down so there is no confusion later.
- **Agree on a Timeline**: Break the project into parts with mini-deadlines. This ensures everyone works steadily rather than leaving everything until the end.
- **Communicate Often**: Have quick check-ins to see how each member is doing. This helps you catch problems early.
- **Address Problems Directly**: If someone is not contributing, talk to them calmly or involve the teacher if it does not improve.
- **Share Success**: If the project goes well, acknowledge each member's effort. This builds positive feelings and reduces future conflicts.

When groups organize themselves well, disagreements over who did the work are less likely to happen. Everyone can do their share and feel valued.

## 6. Bullying vs. Conflict

It is important to distinguish normal peer conflict from bullying. Conflict is a disagreement where both sides can express their views. Bullying is repeated, deliberate harm done by someone with more power—physical strength, social status, or emotional control.

- **Signs of Bullying**: Threats, mean names, spreading false rumors, physically harming someone, or forcing them to do unwanted things.
- **Why It Matters**: Bullying is not just a simple conflict. It is abuse. Victims feel helpless, and the situation might not improve by "talking it out" because the bully aims to control or harm.
- **What to Do**: If you or someone you know faces bullying, tell a teacher, counselor, or administrator. Keep a record of incidents. Bullying often requires adult intervention, consequences for the bully, and support for the target.
- **Standing Up**: If you see bullying, safely speak up or get help. Bystanders who remain silent can make a victim feel even more alone.

While normal conflicts can be solved with negotiation and understanding, bullying needs stronger steps, often involving school policies and protective measures.

---

## 7. Classroom Cliques and Social Circles

Friend groups are a normal part of school, but cliques can form that exclude or look down on others. This can lead to conflicts when:

- **Group Members Disagree**: Within the clique, people might argue about who is the "leader" or who is allowed in.
- **Outside Students Feel Shunned**: They might resent the group for acting superior, possibly leading to teasing or name-calling on both sides.
- **Competition Between Groups**: Groups might clash over resources (like practice areas for clubs) or social events (like deciding who sits where at lunch).

Suggestions for Handling Clique-Related Conflicts

- **Avoid Gossip**: If you are not in the clique, do not spread unkind rumors. If you are in the clique, do not exclude others to feel powerful.
- **Be Kind as an Individual**: Even if your group is negative, you can choose to be welcoming to others.
- **Encourage Group Discussions**: If there is tension among your friends, talk openly about what is bothering each person.
- **Reach Out**: Sometimes, stepping outside your usual circle can help you make new friends and reduce conflicts tied to group identity.
- **Get Adult Help if Needed**: If cliques are causing serious social harm or bullying, a teacher or counselor can help address the underlying issues.

## 8. Using Conflict Resolution in School Settings

Many of the skills covered in earlier chapters—listening, speaking respectfully, finding common ground, and problem-solving—apply directly to school conflicts. Here is a quick reminder:

- **Listen Actively**: Show you care about the other person's viewpoint. Even if you do not agree, hearing them out can reduce anger.
- **Use "I" Statements**: "I feel upset when you do this" instead of "You always ruin everything."
- **Identify Shared Interests**: For classmates, that might be finishing a project well or having a peaceful classroom. For teachers, it could be helping you learn while keeping order.
- **Brainstorm Solutions**: In a group or with a teacher, list several ways to solve the conflict. Then pick the one that seems fair to all.
- **Agree on Next Steps**: Make sure everyone knows what they will do differently.

The more you practice these steps, the more confident you will feel in resolving school arguments. Teachers often encourage such approaches, because a well-managed classroom is better for learning.

## 9. Conflict in Extracurricular Activities

Clubs, sports teams, and other after-school groups are also part of school life. Conflicts can appear here as well:

- **Team Position Disputes**: Players may argue about who should be the star player or who deserves more time in games.
- **Leadership Roles**: Clubs may fight about who becomes president or treasurer.
- **Difference in Commitment**: Some members might want to practice more intensely, while others just want to have fun casually.

**Methods to Address**

- **Clear Criteria**: For sports teams, the coach should set transparent rules on how players are chosen for different positions. For clubs, define how leaders are elected.
- **Team Meetings**: Like family meetings, group discussions can keep everyone on the same page, addressing problems as they arise.
- **Shared Goals**: Remind everyone that the main purpose of a sports team or club is to do well and enjoy the activity. Focusing on this common goal can reduce personal conflicts.
- **Communication with Coaches/Advisors**: If disagreements become serious, involve the adult supervisor who can mediate and set fair guidelines.

---

## 10. Handling Schoolwide Conflicts

At times, an entire school might be split over an issue: changes to the dress code, a new schedule, or a big event being canceled. These larger conflicts can cause heated debates among students, teachers, and administrators.

- **Stay Informed**: Learn the facts about why a change is happening. Sometimes rumors blow issues out of proportion.
- **Use Student Leadership**: Student councils or committees can gather opinions and meet with administrators to find a compromise.
- **Peaceful Discussion**: Organize a town-hall style meeting where everyone can speak or submit questions.

- **Polite Persuasion**: Write respectful letters or emails to the principal or school board, explaining concerns.
- **Respect Decisions**: If, in the end, the school decides on a certain policy, try to follow it calmly unless it violates your basic rights or well-being. You can still politely request changes in the future.

When schools work together to handle large conflicts, it can teach everyone valuable lessons about democracy and collective problem-solving.

---

## 11. Peer Mediation Programs

Some schools have peer mediation, where trained students help others solve disagreements. This can be effective because students might feel more comfortable talking to another student than going to an adult.

**How Peer Mediation Works**

1. **Two Sides Agree to Mediate**: They decide to meet with a neutral mediator.
2. **Mediator Sets Rules**: No interrupting, keep it private, be honest.
3. **Each Side Shares**: The mediator helps them explain their viewpoints and feelings.
4. **Brainstorm Solutions**: The mediator guides them to think of ways to fix the problem.
5. **Agree on a Plan**: Both sign or state a solution they are willing to follow.

Peer mediation can solve many small to medium conflicts before they escalate. However, severe issues like violence or bullying usually require an adult's involvement.

---

## 12. Teacher-Teacher or Teacher-Staff Conflicts

Students may not see it, but teachers can also have conflicts with each other or with school staff. While students might not directly solve these disputes, they can be affected by the stress it causes. Teachers might argue over classroom resources or differ on teaching approaches. School staff might clash over schedules or event planning. In well-managed schools, teachers have their own meetings or speak with administrators to address problems privately, so it does not disrupt student learning.

## 13. Stress and Emotional Reactions at School

School can be stressful due to tests, projects, or personal issues. Stress can make people irritable. Students might snap at each other, or a teacher might be less patient. Recognizing stress signs can help:

- **Know Your Triggers**: If you have a big exam tomorrow, you might be on edge. Avoid heated topics with friends until you are calmer.
- **Take a Break**: If an argument is starting, walk to the hallway or ask for a bathroom pass to breathe and clear your head.
- **Short Chats**: If you need a quick stress release, talk briefly to a supportive friend or a school counselor.
- **Positive Outlets**: Joining a sports team, art club, or simply reading during breaks can reduce stress that leads to conflicts.

## 14. Digital Conflicts and Social Media

School conflicts often continue online after the final bell. Classmates may post unkind comments or gossip on social media. This can grow into cyberbullying or digital harassment.

- **Think Before You Post**: Hurtful words online can be shared widely and quickly.
- **Privacy Settings**: Keep personal details private. This can reduce the chance of being targeted.
- **Avoid Retaliation**: If someone is rude online, responding with insults can escalate it. Instead, block or report them and tell an adult if it is serious.
- **Keep Screenshots**: If threats or bullying occur, screenshots can serve as proof when you report it to the school or a trusted adult.
- **Digital Citizenship**: Schools may teach guidelines on respectful online behavior. Practice them. This helps you and others avoid conflicts.

## 15. Learning from Mistakes

Not every conflict is solved perfectly the first time. You might say the wrong thing or handle a situation badly. That is normal. What matters is learning from the experience:

- **Reflect**: Ask yourself, "What triggered the conflict? Could I have approached it differently?"
- **Apologize If Needed**: If you realize you caused harm, a simple and honest apology can rebuild trust.
- **Adjust for Next Time**: If you learned that texting sarcastic jokes caused a misunderstanding, you might avoid that in the future.
- **Forgive Yourself**: Everyone makes errors. Use the conflict as a lesson to do better.

Being in school means you have a relatively safe space to practice social and communication skills. Overcoming small mistakes can prepare you for bigger challenges later.

---

## 16. When to Seek Adult Help

Sometimes, students try to solve conflicts on their own but hit a wall. Here is when you should talk to a teacher, counselor, or another trusted adult:

- **Physical Threats or Harm**: If you fear someone might get hurt or is already hurting others.
- **Repeated Bullying**: If someone is targeting you or a friend constantly, especially if ignoring them is not working.
- **Serious Harassment**: Threats related to race, religion, gender, or other personal traits.
- **Emotional Distress**: If you or someone else is very upset, crying often, or having trouble focusing because of a conflict.
- **Stolen or Damaged Property**: If someone keeps taking or destroying belongings.

Adults have the authority to enforce school policies and protect students. Do not hesitate to involve them if a situation feels unsafe or too large to handle alone.

## 17. Building a Positive School Culture

Beyond individual conflicts, students can help create a school where conflict is managed well. Some ways to contribute:

- **Model Respect**: Speak kindly, include different people in conversations, and avoid mean jokes.
- **Support Victims**: If you see someone being teased, step in or alert a teacher. Offer friendship or kindness to those who seem alone.
- **Encourage Activities**: Fun events, spirit days, and inclusive clubs can bring students together and reduce negative rivalries.
- **Suggest Peer Workshops**: Propose sessions where students learn about listening skills, handling anger, or appreciating diversity.
- **Be an Ally**: Show you are open to hearing classmates' problems. Sometimes, listening to a friend can prevent their issue from growing into a bigger conflict.

When enough students and staff work toward a caring environment, the entire school benefits. Conflicts still happen, but they are handled faster and more fairly.

---

## 18. Conflict Resolution Clubs or Committees

In some schools, groups of students form conflict resolution clubs. They learn and teach peer mediation, host workshops, or plan events to promote understanding. If your school does not have one, you could talk to a teacher about starting it. The club might do:

- **Peer Mediation**: Train members to help classmates settle disputes.
- **Awareness Campaigns**: Posters or social media messages encouraging kindness.
- **Skill-Building Sessions**: Teach others how to use "I" statements or active listening.
- **Collaborate with Student Council**: Work together on policies that reduce bullying or discrimination.

Such clubs can be a big influence on the overall school climate, showing that students themselves care about peace and respect.

## 19. Handling Conflicts with Kindness and Confidence

School conflict resolution does not require special powers. You can develop skills like empathy, clear communication, and a problem-solving mindset:

- **Stay True to Yourself**: Do not compromise your values just to fit in or avoid conflict. You can disagree politely.
- **Be Brave**: Telling a friend or teacher about serious issues like bullying takes courage. But it can save you or others from harm.
- **Respect Differences**: Not everyone will share your taste in music, style, or humor. That is okay. Focus on cooperation rather than forcing them to be like you.
- **Small Gestures Matter**: A kind comment or a helping hand can create goodwill that prevents future conflicts.
- **Keep Learning**: Each conflict you handle is practice for the next. Over time, you will grow more confident in dealing with challenges.

# Chapter 11: Conflict with Friends

Friendships can be one of the greatest sources of support and happiness. Friends understand our jokes, share our interests, and stand by us when we feel down. But as close as friendships can be, they can also become tense. Friends are not immune to misunderstandings or disagreements. Sometimes, hurt feelings, jealousy, or changes in life can create conflict. When friends have trouble getting along, it can feel scary or sad. Because we care about our friends, we do not want to lose them. Yet, disagreements can happen, even in strong friendships.

In this chapter, we will look at some common causes of conflict between friends and practical ways to address these problems. While some tips from earlier chapters—like listening and speaking respectfully—still apply, we will explore how they fit the special bond between friends. This chapter will also provide ideas on handling issues like trust, honesty, loyalty, and changing interests over time. By learning to navigate conflicts with friends, you can keep those friendships healthy and rewarding.

---

## 1. Why Conflicts Happen Between Friends

It might feel odd that people who like each other can still argue. But friendships involve real human emotions. Friends might:

1. **Spend Lots of Time Together**: If you do many activities with the same person or group, small annoyances can build up.
2. **Feel Strong Emotions**: Caring about someone means you might feel hurt deeply if you think they ignored or betrayed you.
3. **Have Different Goals**: Over time, friends might move in separate directions, leading to tension if they do not respect each other's changing paths.
4. **Expect Loyalty**: If someone does not stand up for you when you are teased, or if they share a secret you told them, it can cause big hurt and conflict.
5. **Face Outside Stress**: Problems at school, work, or home can spill over into friendships, making one or both friends more irritable or sensitive.

When we recognize these sources, we see that conflicts with friends are a normal part of life. The key is learning how to handle them so they do not ruin the friendship or cause lasting resentment.

## 2. Conflict Over Loyalty and Trust

A big part of friendship is trust. We trust friends with our personal details, feelings, and secrets. Conflicts can arise if:

- **Secrets Are Shared**: You tell a friend something private, and they reveal it to others.
- **Friends Take Sides**: Two friends are fighting, and a third friend feels pressured to choose sides.
- **Broken Promises**: A friend says they will do something important for you but never follows through.

**Approach to Handle Loyalty Conflicts**

1. **Speak Up Early**: If a friend shares your secret, do not keep silent and let the hurt grow. Explain calmly how it made you feel.
2. **Ask for Their View**: Maybe they did not realize it was secret or felt compelled by another person. Understanding their reason can lower anger.
3. **Set Clear Boundaries**: If you want something kept private, say so directly: "Please do not share this with anyone."
4. **Decide on Forgiveness**: If the friend is sorry, you might choose to forgive. But if it happens repeatedly, you might keep certain topics to yourself or take a step back from that friendship.

No friendship is perfect, and small slip-ups can happen. What matters is honesty in addressing the betrayal and a willingness to make things right.

---

## 3. Changes in Interests

Friends often form because they share hobbies or routines. But people grow and change. One friend might suddenly take up a new sport, while the other is more into art. Over time, you might notice:

- **Less Time Together**: If your new schedule conflicts with your friend's, you see each other less.
- **Different Conversation Topics**: You might get bored hearing about a hobby you do not like, or they might not share your enthusiasm for new music you found.

- **Feelings of Being Left Out**: If your friend makes new buddies in their new activity, you could feel replaced.

**Ways to Handle Changing Interests**

1. **Respect Their Growth**: Understand that people evolve. Your friend might still care about you, even if they like different things now.
2. **Show Curiosity**: Ask questions about their new interest. You do not have to love it, but learning a bit might help you stay connected.
3. **Invite Them to Join You**: You can still do your favorite activities and invite them along, without pressuring them to say yes every time.
4. **Find Shared Moments**: Even if you do not share all interests anymore, look for smaller things you both enjoy—a certain TV show or a common friend group.
5. **Accept Some Distance**: Sometimes, friendships shift. You can remain friendly and supportive, even if you no longer spend as much time together.

Change can feel scary, but it does not always mean the end of a friendship. With understanding and open communication, friends can adapt to each other's growth.

---

## 4. Feeling Left Out

One of the toughest feelings is the fear of missing out or being excluded. You might see your friend hanging out with someone else. You might hear about a party where you were not invited. This can spark jealousy, sadness, or anger. Conflicts arise if you blame your friend or accuse them of ignoring you.

**Healthy Approaches to Feeling Left Out**

1. **Ask Directly**: If you are unsure why you were not invited, talk calmly to your friend: "I felt hurt that I wasn't included. Is there a reason?"
2. **Check Assumptions**: Sometimes, it was not your friend's event to invite you to, or maybe they thought you would not be interested.
3. **Express Your Wishes**: If you want to be part of certain gatherings, let your friend know you would like an invite next time.

4. **Avoid Confrontations in Anger**: Accusing them—"You like them more than me!"—can push them away. Instead, share your feelings: "I felt sad and worried about our friendship."
5. **Look at Other Friendships**: If one friend group is busy, it can help to build connections elsewhere. Relying on only one friend for social needs can add too much pressure on that relationship.

Though feeling left out is painful, a direct talk can clear up confusion or mistakes. Good friends often appreciate honesty and may not realize how their actions made you feel.

## 5. Small Annoyances That Grow Bigger

Friends may know each other's flaws better than anyone. Maybe your friend talks non-stop, borrows things without returning them promptly, or shows up late again and again. Small habits can grow into arguments if they are never addressed.

**How to Handle Annoyances**

1. **Determine Importance**: Is this habit truly harmful or just a minor annoyance? If it is minor, you might let it go. But if it genuinely upsets you, it is worth discussing calmly.
2. **Speak in Private**: Confronting a friend in front of others can embarrass them. Choose a calm moment to bring up the issue.
3. **Explain the Effect**: "When you are 30 minutes late, I feel disrespected because I have to wait." This helps them see the impact.
4. **Suggest a Fix**: "Could you text me if you think you'll be late, so I can plan accordingly?"
5. **Be Open to Hearing Their Side**: They might have reasons for their behavior or might not even realize how bothersome it is.

Addressing small annoyances quickly helps prevent them from turning into bigger conflicts that can strain or end a friendship.

## 6. Jealousy Between Friends

Jealousy can appear if one friend feels overshadowed by the other's popularity, success, or new relationships. This might look like:

- **Envy of Achievements**: If your friend gets an award or praise, you might feel bad about your own abilities.
- **Comparisons**: Thinking, "Why do they have more money, better clothes, or fun trips?" can create an unspoken bitterness.
- **Clinginess**: One friend might become overly clingy, worried that the other is too busy with new friends.

**Ways to Address Jealousy**

1. **Recognize It**: Admitting to yourself, "I feel jealous because they seem more accomplished right now," can be hard but healing.
2. **Share Your Feelings**: If it is safe to do so, you can gently let your friend know you feel insecure. Sometimes they can reassure you or reduce behavior that triggers your jealousy.
3. **Focus on Your Growth**: Instead of comparing yourself to your friend, look at your own goals and achievements.
4. **Celebrate Their Wins** (Without using the banned term "celebrate"—we can say "acknowledge their wins"): Show genuine support. True friends cheer each other on, even if it stings a bit at first.
5. **Avoid Gossip or Put-Downs**: Speaking badly about your friend's success to others will only create more conflict.

Jealousy is natural, but handling it openly and kindly can help you grow closer rather than pushing you apart.

---

## 7. Dealing with Dishonesty or Harmful Behavior

Sometimes, a friend may lie, manipulate, or act in ways that harm you or others. This is tougher than small annoyances. You might feel betrayed if a friend:

- **Spreads Hurtful Rumors**
- **Steals from You**
- **Pressures You to Do Unhealthy Things**

- Makes Fun of You in Front of Others

**Guidelines for Serious Friend Conflicts**

1. **Confront the Behavior**: Calmly but firmly, say what you have seen or experienced: "I noticed you told people a false story about me."
2. **Ask for an Explanation**: Maybe they were dealing with their own issues. However, do not let them shift blame to you if you know you did nothing wrong.
3. **Draw Boundaries**: If they keep hurting you, step away from the friendship or limit contact. A friendship that consistently harms your well-being is unhealthy.
4. **Seek Support**: Talk to someone you trust—another friend, a family member, or a counselor—if the situation feels too big or upsetting to handle alone.
5. **Stay Safe**: If the friend's behavior involves threats or dangerous actions, report it to an adult. Protecting yourself is more important than protecting the friendship.

While it is tough to walk away from a harmful friend, you deserve respect and safety. A friend who repeatedly acts in harmful ways might not be a true friend at all.

---

## 8. Balancing Friend Groups

Some conflicts arise when you have multiple friend circles that do not get along. For instance, you might have a group from your sports team and another from your art class, and they dislike each other. Or a close friend might not get along with your newer friends.

**Suggestions for Balancing Friend Circles**

1. **Avoid Forcing Them Together**: If two groups clash strongly, accept that they might not all become close with each other.
2. **Spend Time Separately**: Plan hangouts with each group separately to avoid tension.
3. **Clear Communication**: If your friend from group A feels jealous that you hang with group B, let them know you still value them.

4. **Stay Neutral**: Do not carry gossip from one group to another. If they talk badly about each other, encourage them to discuss problems directly or drop the negative talk.
5. **Respect Each Person's Differences**: Being friends with multiple groups can help you grow, as you see different personalities and interests.

Sometimes, it is nice when all your friends get along. But it is not always possible, and it should not force you to pick one group at the expense of another unless something truly unhealthy is happening.

---

## 9. Repairing Friendships After a Fight

Even the best friends can have major blowouts—big disagreements or yelling matches that leave both people feeling hurt. Repairing the friendship requires effort from both sides:

1. **Give Time for Emotions to Cool**: If you are both upset, take a brief break (hours, days) to calm down and think.
2. **Reach Out**: After cooling off, someone has to initiate contact. A short message like, "Could we talk when you're ready?" can open the door.
3. **Own Your Part**: Apologize for specific things you said or did that were hurtful. This shows maturity.
4. **Listen to Their Feelings**: Let them share why they felt hurt. Avoid interrupting or getting defensive right away.
5. **Agree on How to Move On**: Maybe you both decide not to bring up old issues if they are resolved, or you might promise to talk sooner next time conflict arises.
6. **Rebuild Trust**: If trust was broken, it will take time to fix. Consistent kind behavior and honesty help show you truly want the friendship to be strong.

A single apology might not fix everything instantly, but taking these steps can start the healing process.

---

## 10. Knowing When to Let a Friendship End

Not all friendships last forever. It can be painful to accept, but sometimes friends grow so far apart that the relationship becomes tense all the time. If:

- You feel constant anxiety or sadness because of the friendship.
- The friend repeatedly disrespects your boundaries or values.
- You are the only one making efforts to fix problems.

It may be time to step back. This does not have to involve a dramatic fight or cruelty. You can:

- **Reduce Contact**: Speak less often or see each other less.
- **Stay Polite**: You can remain civil if you see them around, without hanging out as closely.
- **Explain Briefly**: If they ask, you can say, "I feel we have different directions in life now. I wish you well, but I need some space."

Though it hurts, letting go of a toxic or worn-out friendship can free both people to grow in healthier ways. Sometimes, after time passes, you might reconnect in a better way. Other times, you may move on and form new bonds that fit who you have become.

---

## 11. Using Humor Carefully

Laughter can defuse tension among friends. A small joke or lighthearted comment might help you both relax if a disagreement is mild. But be careful:

- **Avoid Sarcasm**: If the conflict is serious, sarcasm can sound like mockery.
- **Do Not Dismiss Their Feelings**: Saying "Relax, it's just a joke" when a friend is genuinely upset can make them feel you do not care.
- **Check Their Mood**: If they are very sensitive about a topic, it might be best not to tease about it.
- **Use Self-Deprecation Lightly**: Sometimes joking about your own mistakes can calm things, but do not degrade yourself if it truly hurts your self-esteem.

A gentle, good-natured sense of humor can bring people closer, but it is crucial to read the situation to avoid making the conflict worse.

## 12. Friend Groups Online and Social Media Conflicts

Many friendships continue online through group chats, social media, or gaming communities. Conflicts can happen if:

- **Group Chats Exclude Someone**: A friend may feel left out if they are not invited to a chat or if everyone in the chat jokes about them.
- **Posting Private Information**: Sharing photos or messages that were meant to stay private can cause big betrayal.
- **Public Arguments**: Heated discussions can spill into comment sections, and others might join in to take sides.

**Online Friendship Tips**

1. **Respect Privacy**: Do not post or forward a friend's personal information or pictures without asking.
2. **Use Direct Messages**: If there is a conflict, handle it in private rather than dragging it into a public forum.
3. **Block or Mute if Necessary**: If a friend is harassing you online, you might need to block them for a while to cool the situation.
4. **Speak Face to Face**: Serious issues are often easier to sort out in person or with a phone call, where tone and facial expressions help.
5. **Set Group Chat Rules**: If you have a regular group chat, agree to keep certain topics off-limits or to avoid mocking each other.

Digital communication can quickly turn misunderstandings into bigger rifts. Taking the time to talk offline may save the friendship from damage.

---

## 13. Helping a Friend in Conflict with Someone Else

Sometimes you are not directly involved but see two friends fighting. You might feel stuck in the middle, not wanting to pick sides. Or you might want to help them make peace.

- **Listen to Both**: Let each friend explain their side if they trust you. Avoid judging or sharing one's secrets with the other.
- **Encourage Direct Talk**: Suggest they talk to each other calmly instead of ranting separately to you.

- **Stay Neutral**: If you blame one friend outright, the other might see you as picking sides. Offer to be a mediator if that feels comfortable.
- **Respect Their Choice**: If they are not ready to fix things, do not force them. Sometimes they need time to cool down.
- **Set Boundaries**: If hearing both sides becomes overwhelming, let them know you cannot handle the stress of carrying messages back and forth.

Acting as a supportive listener can help them see each other's perspectives. But do not take on too much. Friendships can have complex dynamics, and it is not always your job to solve others' problems.

---

## 14. Cultural Differences or Backgrounds

Friends from different cultures, beliefs, or backgrounds might misunderstand each other's customs or priorities. This can lead to conflict if:

- **Someone Teases Another's Traditions**
- **They Eat Different Foods and Disagree on Meal Choices**
- **They Have Strongly Different Rules at Home**

**Respecting Differences**

1. **Ask Questions Politely**: Learn about your friend's customs to avoid making wrong assumptions.
2. **Invite Them to Share**: Encourage them to talk about special holidays or routines that matter to them.
3. **Stand Up to Offensive Comments**: If someone outside your friendship circle mocks your friend's background, offer support.
4. **Find Common Values**: Even with cultural differences, you might share a love of music, certain games, or the same sense of humor.

By being respectful, you can avoid turning differences into conflicts. Instead, you might expand your understanding of the world, and your friend can learn about you too.

## 15. Guilt and Unfair Pressure

A friend might pressure you to do something you are not comfortable with. Perhaps they want you to skip class, lie for them, or spend money you do not have. If you say no, they might guilt-trip you by saying you are not a real friend.

**Handling Unfair Pressure**

1. **Know Your Limits**: Be clear with yourself about what you refuse to do—like skipping important tasks or lying to parents.
2. **Stand Firm**: Politely but firmly say, "I'm sorry, but I'm not okay with doing that."
3. **Explain Briefly**: You can add, "I value honesty," or "I can't afford that," but you do not have to make a long defense.
4. **Watch for Manipulation**: If they keep nagging or use emotional blackmail, consider whether this is a respectful friendship.
5. **Offer Alternatives**: Maybe you cannot do what they ask, but you can help in a smaller, honest way. If they refuse that, they might only be looking for someone to do what they want, not a true friend.

Genuine friendships respect boundaries. If a friend punishes you for not breaking your own principles, that is a sign the relationship might be unhealthy.

---

## 16. Building Stronger Bonds After Resolving Conflict

Sometimes, going through conflict with a friend and then resolving it can make your bond stronger. You both learn:

- **How to Address Problems**: Next time something bothers you, you might speak up sooner.
- **Each Other's Boundaries**: You know what they consider sensitive, and they know yours.
- **What Matters Most**: If you both decide the friendship is worth saving, you might treat each other with more care.
- **Better Problem-Solving**: You gain a real example of how to handle tricky situations together.

Though conflict feels stressful, seeing your friendship survive can build deeper trust. You realize you can disagree or mess up and still stay connected if you both try.

## 17. Helping Younger Siblings or Friends with Their Disputes

If you have younger siblings or friends who look up to you, they might come to you when they argue. You can:

- **Show Patience**: Let them share what happened in their own words.
- **Simplify the Situation**: Use easy language to restate the problem: "You wanted to use the same game at the same time, and now you're both upset."
- **Teach Basic Skills**: Simple steps like taking turns, saying sorry, or explaining feelings can go a long way.
- **Encourage Them to Solve It**: Guide them to think of a fair solution rather than giving them the answer.
- **Set an Example**: If they see you handle your own friend issues calmly, they will learn from your actions.

Being a role model for resolving conflicts can help younger people grow up with fewer misunderstandings.

---

## 18. Friendship in Groups or Clubs

In group friendships, conflicts might involve several people:

- **Someone Feels Ignored**
- **Group Jokes at One Person's Expense**
- **Two Friends Disagree, and Others Are Drawn In**

**Ways to Maintain Harmony in a Friend Group**

1. **Group Discussions**: If the issue concerns everyone, talk it out together, letting each person speak.
2. **No Teasing**: Even mild teasing can feel worse in a group setting. Keep jokes kind.
3. **Rotate Roles**: If tasks or responsibilities exist (for instance, in a fan club or online game team), do not always stick one person with the same chore.
4. **Be Inclusive**: Notice if someone in the group is quiet or left out, and invite them to share.

5. **Pair Off**: If two friends keep clashing, suggest they talk in private rather than pulling the whole group into the fight.

Groups can be fun, but they require effort to keep everyone feeling valued and heard.

---

## 19. Preventing Future Friend Conflicts

To reduce the likelihood of conflicts piling up:

1. **Practice Honest Communication**: Share your thoughts in a calm way instead of letting anger build.
2. **Listen Actively**: Show you want to hear their side before jumping in with your own opinion.
3. **Be Reliable**: If you say you will be somewhere at a certain time, try your best to show up. If you borrow something, return it promptly.
4. **Respect Differences**: Friends will not always think or act just like you. Keep an open mind.
5. **Check in Often**: A simple "How are you doing?" can catch problems early. If you sense your friend is distant or upset, kindly ask what is wrong.

While no method guarantees zero arguments, these habits create a positive environment where disagreements are smaller and easier to fix.

---

# Chapter 12: Conflict at Work

For many adults (and even some teens who start part-time jobs), the workplace can become a major setting for daily life. Workplaces bring together people with different backgrounds, roles, and priorities. Conflicts can easily appear over workloads, communication problems, competition for promotions, or personality clashes. Because people rely on work for income and career growth, conflicts here can feel especially tense. In this chapter, we will explore common causes of workplace conflict and how to address them in respectful, professional ways.

---

## 1. Understanding Work Conflict

Work is not just about doing tasks; it is also about interacting with others—coworkers, managers, clients, or customers. Some factors that make workplace conflict likely are:

1. **Team Projects**: Like school group work, employees often have to collaborate with different work styles, and frustration can arise if some are not doing their part.
2. **Performance Pressure**: Deadlines, quotas, or demands from higher-ups can cause stress, making people short-tempered.
3. **Authority Differences**: Managers or supervisors hold power over employees' jobs, pay, and positions. Employees might feel they cannot speak freely if they disagree with a boss's approach.
4. **Resource Competition**: Teams may compete for budgets, office space, or recognition from the company, leading to rivalry.
5. **Personality Clashes**: Different communication styles—some direct, some gentle—can lead to misunderstandings or conflicts.

Conflict at work can impact more than just how people feel. It can reduce productivity, cause employee turnover, and even hurt a business's reputation. That is why handling work conflicts is an essential skill for anyone in the workforce.

## 2. Conflict Between Coworkers

Coworkers at the same level often need to cooperate to achieve shared goals. Conflicts might involve:

- **Uneven Workloads**: One coworker might feel they do extra tasks while the other leaves early or slacks off.
- **Differences in Method**: Disputes over how to complete a project if each person believes their way is better.
- **Personality Friction**: Maybe one is very talkative, another is more private, and they get on each other's nerves.
- **Credit for Work**: If you both worked on a project but only one gets praise or recognition, resentment can grow.

**Strategies to Handle Coworker Conflicts**

1. **Direct Communication**: Politely discuss the issue before it grows bigger. For example, "I noticed you left your tasks unfinished. Can we figure out a fair way to split our duties?"
2. **Stay Professional**: Avoid personal insults or gossip around the office.
3. **Focus on the Goal**: Remind each other that you share the same target—completing tasks well—and see if you can align on that.
4. **Suggest Clear Processes**: If the problem is repeated, propose a schedule or a written plan that outlines who does what.
5. **Involve a Mediator**: If direct talks fail, you might talk to a neutral team leader or HR (Human Resources) staff for help.

Coworker conflicts can often be solved with calm communication, because each side typically wants to maintain a respectful environment and keep their jobs.

---

## 3. Conflict with a Manager or Boss

Having an issue with someone who supervises you can be intimidating. Managers have the power to evaluate performance, approve time off, and influence promotions. Still, they are human and can make mistakes or cause conflict.

- **Unclear Expectations**: If a boss does not give clear instructions or changes them suddenly, workers can become confused and resentful.

- **Unfair Criticism**: Employees may feel singled out or blamed for problems that are not their fault.
- **Lack of Recognition**: People can become discouraged if they never receive positive feedback for hard work.
- **Personality Conflicts**: Some bosses are very strict, while others are more laid back. Employees can clash with either style if it feels disrespectful or ineffective.

**Ways to Address Boss-Employee Conflicts**

1. **Request a Private Meeting**: Calmly say, "I would like to discuss my performance and clarify some points." This shows respect rather than confronting them publicly.
2. **Use Facts, Not Emotions**: If you feel you were treated unfairly, bring specific examples of your work or the situation.
3. **Offer Solutions**: Instead of just complaining, propose a better way to manage tasks or schedules.
4. **Stay Polite but Firm**: Stand up for your rights without being rude. For instance, "I appreciate feedback, but I'd like clearer steps for improvement."
5. **Escalate Carefully**: If the boss is truly unreasonable or harasses you, you might talk to HR or a higher manager. But do this carefully and with evidence.

While a boss holds authority, a good manager should value honest input when delivered in a respectful, solution-focused manner.

---

## 4. Conflict in Team Projects or Departments

Workplaces often have multiple departments or project groups. A conflict can grow between entire teams if they have different goals or budgets. For instance, the marketing team might want to spend more on ads, while the finance team wants to cut costs.

**Team Conflict Tips**

1. **Hold Joint Meetings**: Bring representatives from both sides together to share their needs and limitations.

2. **Clarify Group Goals**: Show how each department's success helps the company overall. If you see you have a shared interest (like profit or customer satisfaction), it can reduce rivalry.
3. **Set Clear Roles**: Decide which team handles which part of a project. Fewer lines get crossed if responsibilities are plainly assigned.
4. **Use Data**: Facts and figures can settle debates that are based on opinion. For instance, if marketing can show that ads will bring in more revenue, finance might see the benefit.
5. **Compromise**: Meeting in the middle—like agreeing on a smaller ad budget but focusing on key areas—can keep both teams satisfied enough to move forward.

When whole departments clash, it can impact many workers. Leaders or senior managers often play a big role in guiding these teams toward cooperation.

---

## 5. Discrimination or Harassment

Sometimes, conflict at work goes beyond simple disagreements and involves unfair treatment based on gender, race, religion, or other personal traits. This is a serious issue. Harassment can appear as jokes, slurs, or repeated unwanted comments or behaviors. Discrimination might show up in promotions, pay, or job assignments.

**Handling Serious Workplace Misconduct**

1. **Document Everything**: Write down dates, times, and exactly what happened or was said.
2. **Report to HR or a Manager**: Most companies have policies against harassment and discrimination. Following the correct steps is crucial.
3. **Seek Support**: Talk to a trusted coworker, friend, or family member about what is happening.
4. **Stay Safe**: If you feel threatened, do not wait—report it to a higher authority or, in very severe cases, contact local law enforcement.
5. **Consider Outside Advice**: Sometimes, talking to a workplace rights group or legal advisor can be necessary if the company ignores the problem.

No one should have to endure harassment at work. Addressing it quickly protects you and may also help others who face similar treatment.

## 6. Work-Life Balance Conflicts

Employees can clash with each other or with managers if one person values personal time highly, while another expects everyone to stay late. Or someone with family obligations might need flexible hours, but the boss demands strict attendance.

**Tips for Work-Life Tensions**

1. **Talk Early**: If you have known obligations (like caring for a relative), explain them when you start the job or as soon as possible.
2. **Negotiate Terms**: Maybe you can come in earlier to leave earlier, or work from home on certain days if the job allows.
3. **Avoid Over-Promising**: Do not promise you can always stay late if that is not true.
4. **Respect Others' Boundaries**: If a coworker says they cannot check email after work hours, do not send repeated late-night messages.
5. **Suggest Company-Wide Policies**: If many employees struggle with the same issue, propose flexible hours or time management training.

Work-life balance helps keep employees healthy, but it can cause conflict if not managed well. Open, respectful dialogue can find solutions that work for both the company and the individual.

## 7. Communication Gaps

Sometimes, a workplace has unclear procedures or relies too much on quick chats rather than formal documentation. Messages might get lost, or instructions can be misunderstood.

- **Missed Emails**: A coworker might say, "I never got the memo," leading to an unfinished task.
- **Vague Directions**: A boss might say, "Do that project quickly," but never define what "quickly" means.
- **Multi-Generational Staff**: Older workers might prefer face-to-face meetings, while younger workers might rely on instant messages or texts.

Bridging Communication Gaps

1. **Clarify in Writing**: After a meeting, send a short email summarizing key points. That way, everyone has a reference.
2. **Use the Right Tools**: If important, email is usually safer than a quick instant message that gets buried. Or use a shared document for tasks, so all can track progress.
3. **Ask for Confirmation**: If you are not sure, ask, "Do I understand correctly that the deadline is next Monday?"
4. **Adapt to the Other Person's Style**: If your manager prefers phone calls, give them a quick ring rather than burying them in messages.
5. **Limit Over-Communication**: Too many messages can also cause confusion. Keep your updates concise and relevant.

Effective communication cuts down on avoidable conflicts and helps everyone focus on their actual work tasks.

---

## 8. Handling Workplace Gossip

Gossip can damage trust within a team. It might start with small talk but grow into rumors that hurt reputations.

- **Why Gossip Happens**: Employees might feel bored, stressed, or curious about others' private lives.
- **Dangers of Gossip**: The person targeted may feel isolated, morale can drop, and the team loses focus on work.

Avoiding or Stopping Gossip

1. **Refuse to Spread It**: If someone shares gossip, do not pass it along. Change the subject or respond neutrally.
2. **Verify Facts**: If you hear a troubling rumor about someone, consider asking them directly or ignoring it unless it is something you must address for work reasons.
3. **Focus on Work Topics**: In the break room, steer conversations toward positive or neutral subjects—sports, cooking, or upcoming company events.

4. **Encourage a Respectful Culture**: A team that values kindness and truth is less likely to engage in harmful gossip.
5. **Confront as Needed**: If you are the subject of gossip, you can calmly address it: "I heard a rumor that I'm leaving the company. That's not true." Then let the gossip fade.

Gossip can be tempting, but staying clear of it helps maintain a professional environment.

---

## 9. Conflict Over Promotions or Raises

When multiple employees aim for a higher position or salary, competition can strain friendships and teamwork.

- **Jealousy**: A coworker might resent you if you get promoted first.
- **Unclear Promotion Criteria**: Employees might suspect favoritism if they do not see a fair process.
- **Arguing Over Credit**: People may fight for the spotlight to improve their chances of a raise or promotion.

**Dealing with Competitive Tension**

1. **Ask About Criteria**: If you want to advance, ask your manager what specific skills or achievements are required.
2. **Focus on Personal Growth**: Improve your own performance rather than tearing others down.
3. **Congratulate Success**: If a coworker gets promoted, give genuine support. You never know when the roles might reverse, and staying gracious keeps relationships healthy.
4. **Collaborate Anyway**: Being seen as a team player can help your reputation more than acting like a lone star.
5. **Suggest Transparent Processes**: If you notice favoritism or confusion, encourage management to post clear job openings, role descriptions, and evaluation steps.

A workplace does not have to turn into a battleground over promotions if employees trust the system and keep respect for each other.

## 10. Bullying or Intimidation in the Workplace

Sadly, bullying is not limited to school. Sometimes, an employee or manager uses intimidation to control coworkers—yelling, belittling them in public, or threatening their job.

**Guidelines to Handle Workplace Bullying**

1. **Document Incidents**: Note what happened, when, and if there were witnesses.
2. **Address It If Safe**: Calmly say, "I do not appreciate being spoken to that way," if you believe it will not put you in danger.
3. **Report to HR**: If bullying continues, show your records to HR.
4. **Build Support**: Talk to others who may also be bullied. There is strength in numbers.
5. **Seek External Help**: If the workplace ignores the problem, you may need legal advice or to look for a new job to protect your well-being.

No job is worth constant abuse. Standing up to bullying can be hard, but it is important for your mental and emotional health.

---

## 11. Cultural and Generational Differences at Work

A modern workplace can have people from various cultures, age groups, and educational levels. Misunderstandings might arise over:

- **Communication Styles**: Some cultures find direct eye contact respectful, others see it as aggressive. Younger workers might use more casual language, older workers might expect formality.
- **Attitudes Toward Hierarchy**: In some cultures, questioning the boss is unacceptable, while in others, it is seen as valuable input.
- **Work Pace**: Some employees believe in quick results; others focus on thorough, methodical steps.

**Embracing a Diverse Workforce**

1. **Learn from Each Other**: Ask questions about preferences and customs in a respectful way.

2. **Avoid Stereotypes**: Do not assume that every older person hates technology or that every younger person is lazy. Judge individuals based on their actual behavior.
3. **Request Training**: Some companies provide diversity and inclusion workshops to help staff understand each other better.
4. **Find Common Goals**: Regardless of background, you share the aim of doing a good job and contributing to the company.
5. **Adapt Where Possible**: You might adjust how you greet or speak to certain coworkers if that helps them feel more comfortable.

Workplace diversity can spark new ideas and insights if everyone treats each other with respect and openness.

---

## 12. Remote or Hybrid Work Conflicts

Many employees now work from home or split time between home and office. This can create unique challenges:

- **Communication Delays**: People in different time zones or home environments might be slower to respond.
- **Lack of Face-to-Face Cues**: In video calls or emails, tone can be misunderstood.
- **Unclear Boundaries**: Some might work late into the night, while others keep strict 9-to-5 hours, leading to confusion about when to contact each other.
- **Tech Problems**: Glitches, lost connections, or outdated software can frustrate team members.

**Improving Remote Work Harmony**

1. **Set Schedules**: Agree on core hours when everyone should be available.
2. **Use Video Wisely**: Video calls can help with more personal connection, but do not overdo them.
3. **Be Clear in Writing**: Because many chats happen via text or email, use short, direct sentences. Summarize key points or requests.
4. **Respect Time Zones**: Avoid scheduling early-morning or late-night meetings if possible.

5. **Stay Patient**: Show understanding when coworkers face home distractions or slow internet.

Remote setups can work smoothly if each person communicates their needs and respects others' situations.

---

## 13. Steps for Addressing Workplace Conflicts

Though each situation differs, a general approach often helps:

1. **Identify the Problem**: Be clear about what is wrong. Is it workload distribution? Miscommunication? Unfair treatment?
2. **Gather Details**: Check emails, recall meetings, and think about specific instances. This helps you present facts.
3. **Request a Private Talk**: Ask the coworker or boss for a time to talk without distractions.
4. **Stay Professional**: Keep your tone calm, avoid personal attacks, and use "I" statements to express concerns.
5. **Suggest Solutions**: Propose a plan or compromise. Ask for their input.
6. **Agree on Next Steps**: Decide who will do what, by when, and how you will measure success.
7. **Follow Up**: Later, check if the solution is working. If not, adjust or involve HR if needed.

Approaching conflict methodically can prevent emotional blowouts and keep the focus on solutions.

---

## 14. Building a Positive Workplace Culture

Companies often talk about "culture"—the shared values and behaviors in an organization. A positive culture does not mean zero conflict; it means people handle conflict respectfully. You can support a healthy culture by:

- **Treating Others Fairly**: Greet people, offer help when possible, and share credit for group achievements.
- **Being Accountable**: If you make a mistake, own it rather than blame someone else.

- **Staying Open to Feedback**: When a coworker or boss points out an error, listen and consider changes without taking it as a personal attack.
- **Volunteering Ideas**: Offer solutions or improvements. Show that you care about the company's well-being, not just your own success.
- **Encouraging Teamwork**: Even if tasks are individual, find moments to collaborate or share advice.

Such actions can reduce conflicts because they create trust and goodwill among colleagues.

---

## 15. Learning from Workplace Conflicts

Even when a conflict is resolved, it is smart to reflect on what went right or wrong:

1. **Review the Cause**: Did you notice early warning signs? Could you have acted sooner?
2. **Check Communication**: Were your emails or comments misunderstood? Next time, how can you be clearer?
3. **Assess Your Own Emotions**: Did you stay calm, or did anger or stress push you to say something unhelpful?
4. **Observe the Outcome**: Did the solution actually solve the root issue, or just hide it? Is the work environment better now?
5. **Plan for Future**: If similar problems arise, you will know to handle them faster or more effectively.

This reflection transforms conflicts from mere stress into valuable lessons for professional growth.

---

## 16. Setting Personal Boundaries at Work

Some conflicts come from not having clear personal boundaries. For instance:

- **Coworkers Who Pry**: Asking private questions about your relationships or finances.
- **Uncomfortable Jokes**: Colleagues making jokes about sensitive topics, expecting you to laugh along.

- **After-Hours Contact**: A boss who sends messages late at night, expecting immediate replies.

**How to Keep Boundaries**

1. **Politely Redirect**: "I prefer not to share details about my personal life at work."
2. **Ignore or Deflect**: If they keep asking, you can change the subject or politely say you need to get back to a task.
3. **Communicate Preferences**: Let your boss or coworkers know if you do not check emails after a certain time.
4. **Stand Firm on Values**: If a coworker's joke offends you, you can say, "I'm not comfortable with that kind of humor."
5. **Escalate If Needed**: If boundaries are repeatedly disrespected, tell a manager or HR.

Boundaries protect your comfort and help maintain a respectful atmosphere.

---

## 17. Conflict Involving Clients or Customers

If your work involves dealing with customers, you might face conflicts with them:

- **Unrealistic Demands**: A customer wants a rush order or an impossible discount.
- **Misunderstandings**: They might have misunderstood a product feature or delivery time.
- **Anger or Rudeness**: Some clients vent frustrations on employees, even if the problem is not the employee's fault.

**Calmly Handling Customer Conflicts**

1. **Listen Patiently**: Let them explain their complaint fully.
2. **Stay Polite**: Keep a calm tone, even if they raise their voice.
3. **Apologize if Justified**: If the company made a mistake, say you are sorry for the inconvenience.
4. **Offer Solutions**: Suggest a refund, a replacement, or other ways to fix the issue if possible.

5. **Know Company Policy**: Understand your organization's rules for returns or refunds so you can act quickly.
6. **Seek Help if Threatened**: If a customer becomes abusive, involve a supervisor or security as needed.

Respectful customer service can turn angry clients into loyal ones and help you feel more in control of tough situations.

---

## 18. Time Management Conflicts

Poor time management can lead to conflict when someone's delays affect the rest of the team. Or a person might overschedule meetings, cutting into coworkers' time for actual work.

- **Missed Deadlines**: Causes extra work for others who must cover or wait.
- **Last-Minute Requests**: Someone suddenly needing help at the end of the day.
- **Unnecessary Meetings**: Wasting everyone's time on details that could be settled via a quick message.

**Reducing Time-Related Tension**

1. **Plan in Advance**: Keep a shared calendar for deadlines, ensuring everyone knows when tasks are due.
2. **Set Priorities**: Let your boss or team know which tasks are top priority.
3. **Limit Interruptions**: Try not to ask coworkers to drop everything for minor requests unless truly urgent.
4. **Speak Up Early**: If you cannot meet a deadline, let people know as soon as possible so they can adjust plans.
5. **Respect Others' Schedules**: If a coworker's busy, see if you can book a short time with them later instead of interrupting their flow.

Clear planning and respect for people's time can drastically cut down on workplace friction.

## 19. When to Seek HR or Higher Management Help

Not all conflicts can be solved by direct communication. Sometimes, an issue is too big, or the person involved is uncooperative.

- **Persistent Harassment or Bullying**: Repeated bad behavior that does not stop after you address it.
- **Rule or Policy Violations**: If a coworker or manager is breaking company rules, ignoring safety standards, or committing fraud.
- **Strong Personality Clashes**: If talks lead nowhere and the conflict disrupts the entire team.
- **Health or Safety Risks**: Any conflict that endangers your well-being or that of others.

**What HR or Management Can Do**

1. **Investigate**: Talk to both sides to understand the facts.
2. **Mediate**: Lead a structured conversation where each side presents their viewpoint.
3. **Apply Company Policy**: If someone violated rules, HR can enforce consequences.
4. **Suggest Transfers**: If two people cannot work together, sometimes one can move to a different team.
5. **Protect Confidentiality**: HR should keep your report confidential as much as possible.

Involving HR or upper management is a serious step. It can help resolve big issues that you cannot fix on your own.

# Chapter 13: Respect and Empathy

Respect and empathy are two key traits that can keep conflicts from growing. When people treat each other kindly and try to see things from the other person's perspective, it becomes easier to solve problems. Without respect, conversations can turn into personal attacks. Without empathy, we might ignore someone else's feelings and make the conflict worse. In this chapter, we will explore what respect and empathy look like in different settings, why they matter so much, and how to grow these qualities in our daily lives. By the end, you will see how respect and empathy can prevent arguments from escalating, help you connect better with others, and bring more understanding into almost any disagreement.

## 1. Defining Respect

**Respect** means treating someone like they matter. It involves seeing that they are a person with their own thoughts, feelings, and rights. It is not about always agreeing or admiring everything about them. Rather, it is about honoring their human worth. When we give respect, we use polite language, avoid insults, and refrain from behaviors that belittle the other person. Even if we disagree strongly with their ideas, we do not see them as worthless or unimportant.

- **Respect for Rules or Customs**: In groups or families, respect can show up when people follow shared rules. This might be as simple as not interrupting when someone else is speaking.
- **Respect for Personal Space**: This involves not touching someone's belongings without asking, not barging into their room, or not standing too close if that makes them uneasy.
- **Respect for Time**: Not making someone wait endlessly, or being mindful of deadlines and appointments.
- **Respect for Boundaries**: Recognizing that each person has limits—be they emotional, physical, or mental—and choosing not to push them in harmful ways.

When conflict arises, respect remains crucial. Even if you are frustrated, keeping a respectful tone and not resorting to name-calling or threats helps keep the conversation calmer. Disagreements without respect quickly spiral into arguments where each side just wants to "win" or hurt the other. But disagreements with respect can lead to solutions where both sides feel heard.

## 2. Defining Empathy

**Empathy** means understanding how someone else feels. It does not mean you have to feel their emotion exactly or fix their problems for them. Empathy simply involves imagining yourself in their situation enough to sense what they might be going through. This skill makes conflicts easier to manage because it lowers the urge to judge or dismiss the other person's emotions.

- **Cognitive Empathy**: You understand the thoughts behind someone's feelings. For example, your friend is angry because they lost an important game, and you see how that frustration makes sense to them.
- **Emotional Empathy**: You feel a bit of their emotion. Maybe you become sad when you watch a friend cry about a family issue because you share their sadness.
- **Compassion**: You want to help lessen their pain or confusion. This does not mean taking responsibility for their entire life, but you care enough to offer comfort or a listening ear.

Empathy leads us to speak more kindly and listen more fully. In a conflict, if you see that the other person is stressed or scared, you might respond with patience instead of snapping back. Even if you believe they are partly at fault, empathy reminds you that they are a person with feelings. This can keep you from hurting them further. When both sides show empathy, conflicts are much more likely to be solved fairly.

---

## 3. How Respect and Empathy Reduce Conflict

You might wonder why respect and empathy are so frequently mentioned as vital traits in disagreement. The answer lies in how they affect communication:

1. **They Calm Emotions**: When you speak respectfully and show empathy, the other person feels safer and less defensive. This helps them talk without yelling or shutting down.
2. **They Encourage Openness**: People who feel respected are more likely to share their real concerns. They sense that you will not mock or dismiss them. As a result, deeper issues come to the surface, allowing for more honest problem-solving.

3. **They Lower the Desire for Revenge**: If someone sees that you genuinely care about how they feel, they are less likely to want to retaliate or "get even."
4. **They Show Goodwill**: Respect and empathy show that you want a positive result, not a victory at all costs. This can motivate the other side to also meet you halfway.
5. **They Prevent Escalation**: Disagreements can turn ugly when insults fly and people feel attacked. Respectful language and empathy act like a safety net, keeping arguments on a humane level.

Imagine two coworkers who have a scheduling conflict. If they start by respecting each other's time and empathizing with each other's workloads, they can often find a solution faster. By contrast, if one coworker says, "You're so lazy for not coming early," it provokes anger. Then the conflict becomes personal rather than about scheduling.

---

## 4. Showing Respect in Everyday Interactions

It is easier to keep respect in big disagreements if you practice it daily. Here are some common ways:

- **Listening Without Interrupting**: Give people space to finish their thoughts before you jump in.
- **Using Courteous Language**: Words like "please" and "thank you" do not solve conflicts on their own, but they set a friendly tone.
- **Accepting Differences**: Not everyone thinks as you do. Respect means acknowledging those differences without mocking them.
- **Keeping Promises**: When you promise someone you will show up or help, following through shows you value their time and trust.
- **Avoiding Gossip**: Talking badly behind someone's back shows disrespect. It also makes people doubt whether you respect them when they are not around.

These small habits build a general culture of respect. So when a conflict arises, it does not start from a place of tension. People already see you as someone who behaves honorably.

## 5. Developing Empathy Through Practice

Some people feel empathy comes naturally, while others need more practice. Either way, you can get better at it by doing the following:

- **Listen Actively**: Try to understand not just the words someone says, but their underlying feelings. Are they stressed, sad, or worried?
- **Ask Questions**: Politely ask for more detail about why they feel a certain way. For example, "You seem upset. Can you tell me more about what is bothering you?"
- **Reflect Their Feelings**: If someone says, "I'm frustrated because nobody listens to me at home," you might respond, "It sounds like you feel ignored, and that must be tough." This lets them know you grasp their experience.
- **Try Imagining Their Situation**: If you had their job, family, or daily life, would you feel similarly? Even a few seconds of imagining their background can open your mind.
- **Check Assumptions**: Often, we guess someone's motives without asking. "He's probably late because he's lazy," might be one guess. But real empathy would check if he had a rough commute or personal emergency.
- **Recognize Shared Humanity**: No matter the differences in age, culture, or beliefs, every person has hopes and worries. Seeing that common ground helps empathy grow.

When empathy is strong, you become more thoughtful about how your words or actions affect others. This can stop many conflicts from arising in the first place, since you avoid careless or hurtful behavior.

---

## 6. Balancing Respect and Honesty

Some people worry that showing too much respect or empathy might make them a pushover. They fear they will have to agree with everything the other person says. However, that is not true. You can remain honest and direct while still keeping respect for them as a person.

- **Speak Truthfully but Kindly**: If a coworker's idea is not practical, you can say, "I see why you think this idea might work, but here is why I have concerns," instead of "That's a dumb plan."

- **Set Boundaries**: You can respect someone and feel empathy for them, but also firmly say "no" to demands that hurt you or go against your principles.
- **Encourage Two-Way Respect**: Respect is not letting others walk all over you. It is about mutual courtesy. If they do not offer the same respect in return, you can speak up or limit how you interact.
- **Speak About Behavior, Not Character**: If you are giving feedback, point out specific actions rather than insulting them as a person. "I felt disrespected when you shouted at me in front of others" is better than "You're a horrible person."

By combining honesty with thoughtfulness, you maintain integrity without stepping on someone else's dignity.

## 7. The Role of Respect in Cultural Differences

In some conflicts, cultural backgrounds can clash. A gesture that is polite in one culture might be offensive in another. Respect here means learning or asking about the other person's norms. For example, in some places:

- **Direct Eye Contact** might show confidence, while in others, it might be seen as rude.
- **Physical Space** might vary; some cultures stand close when talking, while others prefer distance.
- **Greetings** can differ widely—some cultures use handshakes, others bow, and others might not touch at all.

When you travel or meet someone from a different background, a quick show of curiosity—such as, "What's the best way to greet you?"—demonstrates respect. This can avoid unintentional conflict that arises purely from cultural misunderstandings.

Similarly, empathy helps you see that their way of doing things is tied to upbringing or local norms. Instead of dismissing them as "weird," empathy encourages you to understand the reasons behind their customs.

## 8. Respecting Those with Opposing Views

Life is full of disagreements over politics, religion, or personal values. In such debates, respect often disappears quickly. People feel attacked when their core beliefs are challenged. However, it is entirely possible to disagree strongly and remain respectful. How?

1. **Avoid Mockery**: Laughter at someone's deeply held view leads to anger, not understanding.
2. **Use "I" Statements**: "I believe this because…" is less aggressive than "You are wrong."
3. **Ask Sincere Questions**: "I'd like to know more about why this is important to you," shows you are willing to listen.
4. **Check for Shared Values**: Maybe you both want a better community, but you disagree on how to get there. Realizing the shared goal can reduce tension.
5. **Know When to End It**: If the talk is going nowhere, respectfully say, "We may have to agree to disagree on this."

This approach keeps lines of communication open. People are more likely to respect your views if they see you treating them with respect.

---

## 9. Empathy in Conflict Resolution Sessions

In formal conflict resolution settings—like mediation or counseling—empathy can be a structured part of the process. For example:

- **Each Party Gets to Speak**: They share how they feel and why.
- **The Other Side Reflects**: They repeat back what they heard, ensuring they understand the feelings and content correctly.
- **Listeners Acknowledge**: "I see how that must have been frustrating for you," or "I understand why you might feel hurt."
- **Seeking Common Ground**: Once feelings are recognized, it is easier to find solutions that honor each side's needs.

This might seem slow compared to arguing, but it prevents harm. By spending time on empathy, the final agreement is often stronger and longer-lasting, because both parties feel genuinely heard.

## 10. Self-Respect and Self-Empathy

Respect and empathy must also extend inward—toward yourself. Self-respect means you value your own well-being enough not to accept rude treatment or belittling from others. Self-empathy means you recognize your own feelings and treat yourself with kindness.

- **Setting Boundaries**: If someone continually disrespects you, self-respect says you may distance yourself or seek help if they refuse to stop.
- **Self-Kindness**: If you make a mistake, self-empathy avoids harsh self-criticism. Instead, you acknowledge your disappointment but also accept your humanity.
- **Refusing Unfair Blame**: In conflicts, some people might try to pin everything on you. Self-respect means checking the facts and not taking full blame for things beyond your control.
- **Caring for Your Mental Health**: Sometimes, you need to step back, rest, or seek professional support if conflicts become too heavy.

When you hold healthy self-respect, you are better at showing genuine respect to others, because you are not acting out of low self-worth or desperation to be liked.

---

## 11. Teaching Respect and Empathy to Children

Children learn by example. If they see adults handling conflicts respectfully and with empathy, they are more likely to mimic that behavior. Parents, teachers, and caregivers can help children by:

- **Modeling Good Language**: Use polite words and a calm tone when correcting a child's mistake. They notice whether we practice what we preach.
- **Role-Playing**: Ask them, "How would you feel if someone took your toy without asking?" This helps them imagine the other side's emotions.
- **Praised for Kindness**: Notice and thank them when they show empathy or respect, such as sharing a snack with a friend or waiting patiently.
- **Explaining Consequences**: When a child is mean, calmly help them see that the other child feels sad or hurt. This builds empathy.
- **Encouraging Apologies**: Even a simple "I'm sorry" can teach them to take responsibility for hurting someone, while also learning to forgive and move on.

Raising children in an environment where respect and empathy are normal prepares them to handle future conflicts in healthier ways.

## 12. Overcoming Barriers to Respect

Some people struggle to show respect if they grew up in harsh environments or were taught to see others as rivals. In many cases:

- **Past Hurts**: They might have been disrespected themselves, so they learned to be defensive.
- **Cynicism**: They believe no one is honest or worthy of trust.
- **Anger at Authority**: They might see any form of courtesy as submission.

Breaking these patterns takes time, but it is possible:

1. **Therapy or Counseling**: A counselor can help someone recognize why they find it hard to treat others with respect, then work on better habits.
2. **Positive Role Models**: Spending time around people who consistently act kindly can show that respect is not weakness but strength.
3. **Small Steps**: Start with polite words in everyday moments, like with a store clerk or bus driver, and gradually expand this courtesy to bigger conflicts.
4. **Learning to Trust**: As they see that respectful behavior often leads to better outcomes, their belief in respect can grow.

It is not an overnight change, but repeated efforts can unlearn rude or dismissive habits, replacing them with genuine respect.

## 13. Overcoming Barriers to Empathy

Likewise, some people find it tough to empathize. They might:

- **Be Very Focused on Themselves**: They rarely pause to consider others' perspectives.
- **Have Experienced Trauma**: Sometimes, shutting down empathy is a way they learned to protect themselves.

- **Lack Exposure**: They have not spent time hearing diverse stories or meeting people with different struggles.
- **Fear Being Overwhelmed**: They worry that feeling someone else's pain will be too distressing.

To improve empathy:

1. **Listen to Personal Stories**: Reading books or articles where people share real experiences, especially those unlike your own, can expand your sense of empathy.
2. **Volunteer or Community Work**: Seeing others' challenges up close—like helping in shelters—can open your heart.
3. **Mindful Observation**: Notice body language, tone, and expressions. These give clues about someone's inner state.
4. **Patience**: Do not rush yourself. If empathy feels awkward at first, keep trying gently. Over time, it becomes more natural.

Even if you are not naturally empathetic, you can still learn to respond with kindness and a willingness to understand.

---

## 14. Conflict Scenarios Where Respect and Empathy Make a Difference

Let's explore a few short examples:

1. **Sibling Argument Over TV**: Two siblings want to watch different shows. If they roll their eyes and call each other names, the fight escalates. But if one says, "I know you love that show, and I get why you want to watch it now," they are showing empathy. Then maybe the other sibling replies, "I appreciate you understand that. Maybe we can take turns tonight," showing respect for each other's wishes.
2. **Coworker Takes Credit for Your Idea**: You feel angry and want to shout at them. If you approach them with respect—"I'm concerned because it seemed like you presented my idea as your own. Can we talk about how to handle credit more fairly?"—they might respond better than if you publicly accuse them. Empathy would also try to see if they felt pressured or fearful about their own performance.
3. **Parent-Teen Conflict Over Rules**: The teen might say, "I feel suffocated by a 9 PM curfew," while the parent might fear for the teen's safety.

Empathy helps the teen see the parent's worry, and respect helps the parent treat the teen's need for freedom seriously. They might find a compromise if both sides stay calm.
4. **Friends with Different Values**: One friend is very environmentally conscious, the other is less focused on it. Respect means not mocking the "green" friend as oversensitive, and empathy means trying to see why they feel strongly about protecting nature. Even if the second friend does not fully change, they might show courtesy, such as recycling more often to respect the friend's concerns.

In each scenario, conflicts are minimized or solved because the people involved use respect to keep the tone civil and empathy to grasp each other's feelings.

---

## 15. Empathy vs. Agreement

One confusion people sometimes have is thinking empathy means agreeing with the other person. That is not the case. You can empathize with someone—truly see their point of view—yet still hold a different opinion. For instance:

- **Teacher vs. Student**: The student empathizes that the teacher wants order in the classroom, yet they still believe the teacher's punishment was too harsh. They respect the teacher's role but disagree on the severity.
- **Health Choices**: A friend might choose to eat junk food. You empathize that they find it comforting, but you disagree that it is the best choice.
- **Political Views**: You can fully understand why someone supports a certain policy (maybe it benefits their hometown), yet you do not support that policy yourself.

Empathy just means you get why they think or feel that way. It does not cancel your own stance. This distinction helps keep you from feeling forced to "give in" just because you care about the other person's feelings.

---

## 16. Harnessing Respect and Empathy in Group Conflicts

When a group—like a club or committee—disagrees, conflict can get messy. Respect and empathy help keep group morale steady:

- **Structured Sharing**: Each member speaks in turn while everyone else listens. This enforces respect.

- **Reflective Responses**: After someone speaks, another member restates what they heard, showing empathy.
- **Fair Attention**: Avoid letting one loud voice dominate. Respect for all members means each has time to speak.
- **Common Purpose**: Remind the group of shared goals, like finishing a project or improving the club. When they see they are on the same team, empathy and respect become easier to show.
- **No Mocking**: If someone's idea seems off, politely explain concerns. Do not belittle them in front of everyone.

Groups that practice these habits can have lively debates without hurting relationships.

## 17. Rebuilding Respect After It's Broken

Sometimes, respect is lost. Maybe you lashed out at someone with harsh words. Or they did something that really hurt you, and you no longer see them in a positive light. Rebuilding respect is possible but takes effort:

1. **Sincere Apologies**: If you were the one who disrespected them, own it. "I realize my words were rude. I'm sorry for that."
2. **Proven Change**: Words alone are not enough. Over time, show through actions that you can be considerate.
3. **Understanding the Causes**: If they hurt you, try to see if it was a mistake, misunderstanding, or repeated behavior. Sometimes, empathy for their situation can soften your anger. But if it is a pattern, keep boundaries.
4. **Gradual Trust**: Respect can return step by step, not instantly. If trust was shattered, smaller positive interactions can slowly heal the wound.
5. **Seek Mediation**: If direct efforts fail, a neutral third party might help both sides talk fairly.

Though it is easier to keep respect than to repair it after it breaks, it is still worth trying, especially if the relationship matters.

## 18. When Empathy Feels One-Sided

At times, you might be the one showing empathy, but the other person does not reciprocate. They may:

- **Dismiss Your Feelings**
- **Laugh at Your Efforts to Understand Them**
- **Refuse to Listen**

Here, it is crucial to remember a few points:

- **You Control Only Your Actions**: You cannot force someone else to empathize.
- **Protect Your Well-Being**: If they are hostile, limit how much personal harm you take. Setting boundaries is wise.
- **Stand Firm in Your Values**: Keep being respectful and empathetic to the degree you can. Do not let their behavior drag you into rudeness.
- **Decide on Future Interaction**: If they consistently refuse mutual respect, consider reducing contact or seeking help from a supervisor, mediator, or counselor if needed.

Empathy is powerful, but it works best when both parties engage. If not, at least you have the satisfaction of knowing you tried your best to keep the conversation civil.

---

## 19. Small Daily Actions That Strengthen Respect and Empathy

Even outside of conflict, you can strengthen these traits in everyday life:

1. **Thank People**: Whether it is the cashier or a friend who held the door, acknowledging someone's small help is a sign of respect.
2. **Offer a Listening Ear**: When a family member talks about their day, really tune in rather than nodding while scrolling your phone.
3. **Practice Kind Words**: Compliment coworkers or classmates on good work. A short, honest compliment builds a spirit of respect.
4. **Share Others' Joys or Struggles**: If a friend is excited about an achievement or worried about a problem, show you care. This is empathy in action.
5. **Reflect Before Responding**: If someone says something you dislike, take a brief moment to consider what they might be feeling before reacting.

These small habits make respect and empathy a normal part of your interactions, so that when a real conflict hits, you have a strong foundation to build on.

# Chapter 14: Handling Anger

Anger is a strong emotion that can appear quickly when you feel threatened, hurt, or frustrated. Everyone experiences anger from time to time. It is a normal part of human emotion, signaling that something feels wrong. However, when anger takes control, it can lead to shouting, name-calling, or even physical fights—actions that harm relationships and make conflicts worse. Learning how to handle anger in constructive ways can help you remain calm, communicate more effectively, and find better solutions to disagreements.

In this chapter, we will look at what anger is, why it occurs, and methods to manage it so that it does not harm you or others. These tools can help both children and adults keep anger from overwhelming them, leading to safer, more respectful conflict resolution.

---

## 1. Understanding Anger

Anger is often called a "secondary emotion," because it usually follows a more vulnerable feeling like sadness, fear, or shame. For example, you might feel embarrassed if someone teases you in front of your peers, and that embarrassment can quickly shift into anger. Or you might feel afraid of losing something important, and that fear becomes anger directed at a person you blame.

- **The Physical Side of Anger**: You might notice increased heartbeat, tight muscles, sweating, or a rush of energy. Your body prepares for "fight or flight," which once helped humans handle threats.
- **The Mental Side**: Angry thoughts can arise, such as "This is unfair!" or "They always disrespect me!"
- **The Behavioral Side**: You may feel the urge to yell, throw things, or become sarcastic.

Recognizing these signals is the first step. Once you notice you are getting angry, you can take steps to manage it before it intensifies.

---

## 2. Common Triggers for Anger

People have different anger triggers, but some common ones include:

- **Feeling Disrespected**: If you believe someone is insulting you, ignoring you, or treating you unfairly, anger often results.
- **Blocked Goals**: You have a plan or desire, but someone or something stands in your way. For instance, a sudden car problem when you are late for work.
- **Frustration from Repeated Problems**: If the same issue keeps happening—like a sibling taking your things—anger can build up over time.
- **Betrayal or Broken Trust**: A friend who shares your secret or a coworker who takes credit for your work can spark strong anger.
- **Stress and Exhaustion**: When you are already tired or overwhelmed, small annoyances might set you off.
- **Perceived Threat**: You might feel physically unsafe or worry about losing status or relationships, making you defensive and angry.

Knowing your personal triggers helps you prepare for them. If, for example, you realize you get angry when hungry, you can watch for that warning sign and find a snack before snapping at someone.

---

## 3. The Harmful Effects of Uncontrolled Anger

Anger in itself is not evil. It is a message that something is off. The real problem is when anger becomes uncontrollable:

1. **Damaged Relationships**: Yelling, insulting, or physically lashing out breaks trust and can push people away, whether they are friends, family, or coworkers.
2. **Regretful Words**: In anger, you might say hurtful things you do not actually mean. Apologizing later might help, but the wound can linger.
3. **Poor Decisions**: Anger narrows your thinking. You might act impulsively, making choices that harm your future or your job.
4. **Stress on the Body**: Chronic anger or frequent rage episodes can lead to health problems like high blood pressure or sleeplessness.

5. **Unresolved Issues**: Instead of focusing on solving the conflict's cause, uncontrollable anger focuses on hurting or blaming the other side, leaving the real problem untouched.

Thus, learning to manage anger is not about ignoring it. Rather, it is about listening to the message it sends, then responding wisely.

---

## 4. Recognizing Early Warning Signs

Catching anger early gives you the best chance of calming down before losing control. Common clues include:

- **Physical Tension**: Tight jaw, clenched fists, or a flushed face.
- **Fast Heartbeat or Breathing**: As your body readies for action, you might sense a surge of energy.
- **Racing Thoughts**: Your mind floods with complaints about how unfair the situation is.
- **Desire to Escape or Attack**: You might want to leave the room or confront someone immediately.
- **Irritability**: Small things that usually do not bother you start feeling huge.

If you notice these, it is a signal to put anger management tools into action right away. Waiting until you are in full-blown rage makes calm resolution much harder.

---

## 5. Basic Anger Management Techniques

There are many ways to calm anger. Here are some well-known methods:

1. **Deep Breathing**: Take slow, deep breaths, inhaling for a count of four, pausing, and exhaling for a count of four. Repeat until you feel the tension ease.
2. **Count to Ten**: A classic technique to pause before reacting. Silently count from one to ten (or higher) if needed. This break can prevent impulsive actions.

3. **Grounding**: Focus your senses on the present moment—feel your feet on the floor, notice three things you see in the room, and listen for sounds around you. This lowers the intensity of anger by shifting attention.
4. **Positive Self-Talk**: Remind yourself, "I can stay calm. I'll handle this better if I don't shout." Repeating simple, encouraging words can counter angry thoughts.
5. **Take a Time-Out**: Step away from the situation for a few minutes. Let the other person know you need a brief pause to cool off. This is not running away; it is a strategic break to avoid escalation.

These simple techniques interrupt anger's momentum. You can pick whichever strategy feels most natural and practice it until it becomes a habit.

---

## 6. Long-Term Anger Control Methods

Beyond immediate tactics, you can also work on your anger response over time:

- **Regular Exercise**: Physical activity like running, dancing, or sports helps release tension and lowers baseline stress.
- **Healthy Sleep**: Exhaustion can make anger flare up quickly. Aim for consistent, restful sleep.
- **Journaling**: Writing about your feelings and daily triggers helps you see patterns. You may spot the same issues making you angry, prompting solutions.
- **Counseling or Therapy**: If anger is frequent and intense, a professional can help you find deeper reasons (like past trauma) and teach personalized strategies.
- **Relaxation Practices**: Meditation, yoga, or breathing exercises done daily can make you calmer overall, less prone to sudden rage.

Building these long-term habits strengthens your emotional resilience, so anger does not overwhelm you as often.

---

## 7. Communicating Anger Constructively

Some people think they must either hold in anger or explode. But there is a middle path—expressing anger in a calm, clear way:

1. **Use "I" Statements**: Say, "I feel upset when you raise your voice," rather than "You make me angry by yelling."
2. **Be Specific**: Explain what bothers you rather than attacking the person. "I felt disrespected when you interrupted me," is clearer than "You're always so rude."
3. **Propose Solutions**: If possible, suggest how the situation can improve. "Could we agree to take turns speaking so neither feels cut off?"
4. **Stay Respectful**: Keep a moderate tone. Avoid sarcasm, name-calling, or blaming.
5. **Allow Them to Respond**: Ask for their perspective. If you express anger calmly, they are more likely to share their side instead of just defending themselves.

This approach handles anger without ignoring it or letting it run wild. It may feel awkward at first if you are used to venting anger. But with practice, it becomes a healthier way to stand up for yourself.

---

## 8. Teaching Children Anger Management

Kids often have strong bursts of anger but less ability to control it. Guiding them can prevent habits like hitting or screaming:

- **Name the Feeling**: Help them put words to their emotion—"You seem angry right now," so they start recognizing it.
- **Model Calm Behavior**: If a parent or teacher yells in anger, children learn that response. Show them steady, calm ways of handling frustration.
- **Simple Techniques**: Teach them to take a few deep breaths, count to ten, or use a calm-down corner.
- **Praise Good Effort**: If they handle anger better than before, notice that improvement. "I'm proud you took a break instead of yelling."
- **Set Clear Rules**: Explain that hitting or name-calling is not allowed. Offer acceptable ways to express anger, like using words or drawing a picture.

Early guidance can shape them into adults who know how to manage anger without causing harm to themselves or others.

## 9. Dealing with Someone Else's Anger

What if you are the target of another person's anger? It can be scary or intimidating. Some tips:

1. **Stay Composed**: If you can, keep your voice calm and your body language nonthreatening.
2. **Listen if Possible**: Sometimes, people calm down if they feel heard. But if they are yelling nonstop, you might need to suggest a pause.
3. **Do Not Fuel It**: Resist the urge to mock or challenge them aggressively. That often escalates the anger.
4. **Set Boundaries**: If they start insulting or getting too close physically, you can say, "I want to talk, but not if you threaten me."
5. **Seek Help**: If you feel unsafe, leave the situation and find help. Do not try to handle violent or extreme anger alone.

Dealing with someone else's anger is not about letting them walk all over you. It is about keeping yourself safe and, if possible, guiding the situation toward calm conversation.

---

## 10. Anger vs. Assertiveness

Anger sometimes masquerades as assertiveness, but they are not the same:

- **Assertiveness**: Standing up for your rights or expressing your needs while respecting others. You remain polite but firm.
- **Aggression**: Using anger, threats, or force to get your way, often disregarding the rights or feelings of others.

Conflicts often call for assertiveness: you state what bothers you and what you want, but in a tone that does not demean the other side. Aggression, on the other hand, provokes fear or resentment and rarely leads to lasting solutions.

---

## 11. Cultural Views on Anger

Different cultures have varied norms on expressing anger. Some encourage people to vent openly, while others expect them to keep anger private. These differences can cause misunderstandings. For instance, someone from a more expressive background might seem aggressive to a more reserved person. Meanwhile, someone raised to hide anger might seem "fake" or "passive" to someone from a direct culture.

In cross-cultural conflicts, acknowledging these differences helps reduce confusion:

- **Ask About Preferences**: If you are unsure, you can politely say, "Is it okay to share direct feelings here, or would you prefer a private setting?"
- **Notice Body Language**: Sometimes, anger is shown subtly, like avoiding eye contact or stiff posture.
- **Stay Curious**: Rather than assuming they are "rude" or "weak," consider their cultural norms around anger expression.

Understanding these nuances can make it easier to handle disagreements without disrespecting each other's backgrounds.

---

## 12. Handling Anger in Group Conflicts

When multiple people are angry, the energy can escalate quickly. Strategies to contain group anger include:

- **Designated Speaker**: Let each person speak in turn, so nobody shouts over anyone else.
- **Group Agreement on Civility**: Before discussing a hot topic, the group can agree on a rule: no insults or yelling.
- **Mediation**: A neutral mediator can guide the process, ensuring everyone's voice is heard but not overshadowed by anger.
- **Breakout Sessions**: If the group is large, smaller groups can talk first and calm heated emotions before reconvening.
- **Focusing on Shared Goals**: Reminding everyone why they gather (a project, a team victory, or a community event) can refocus them away from personal anger.

Group anger, if not addressed, can lead to chaos or splits. But with clear guidelines and a willingness to pause, it can be managed.

## 13. Digital Anger: Online Arguments

On social media or online forums, anger can flare up quickly. Miscommunication is easier without tone or facial expressions. People might say things online they would never say in person.

- **Pause Before Replying**: If you see a comment that enrages you, wait. Type a draft but do not send it yet. Cool off, then decide if you still want to post.
- **Avoid Personal Attacks**: Stick to the topic, not the person.
- **Private Conversation**: If possible, take the conflict to direct messages or a phone call, where tone can be clearer and less public.
- **Know When to Stop**: Online debates often escalate without resolution. If it becomes a loop of anger, step away.
- **Use Neutral Language**: Words can appear harsher online, so choose calmer phrasing to avoid unintended offense.

Since online conflicts can escalate quickly, controlling anger in digital spaces requires extra caution.

---

## 14. Channeling Anger into Positive Action

Sometimes, anger can be a motivator for change. If you are angry about an injustice, you might join a community group that addresses it. If you are angry about a personal habit that is harming you, that anger might spur you to change.

- **Identify the Source**: What exactly are you angry about? Is it something that can be changed or improved?
- **Brainstorm Solutions**: Ask, "What can I do to fix or reduce this problem?" rather than just venting.
- **Collaborate With Others**: Teaming up with people who share your concern can channel anger into organized effort.
- **Stay Constructive**: Even if the cause is serious, use anger as energy, not as a weapon.
- **Measure Progress**: Keep track of improvements so you do not get stuck in endless rage.

This approach transforms anger from a destructive force into a spark for growth.

## 15. Self-Talk to Manage Anger

The thoughts in our heads often fuel anger or calm it. Notice the things you tell yourself during a conflict:

- **Negative Self-Talk**: "They're doing this on purpose to make me miserable," or "This always happens to me." This intensifies anger and frustration.
- **Balanced Self-Talk**: "They might not realize how their actions affect me. I can explain it calmly," or "I'm upset, but I'll handle it better if I stay respectful."

By replacing negative self-talk with more balanced messages, you steer your anger away from destructive behavior. It takes practice, but it can dramatically reduce heated outbursts.

## 16. Apologies and Rebuilding After Anger

Despite best efforts, anger might still get the better of you sometimes. You may snap at a friend or coworker or send a harsh message in the heat of the moment. In these cases:

1. **Own Up to It**: Acknowledge your outburst or harsh words.
2. **Apologize Honestly**: "I'm sorry for yelling at you. I was overwhelmed, but that's not an excuse for my behavior."
3. **Explain Briefly**: You can share you were upset about something, but do not shift blame entirely onto them.
4. **Commit to Change**: "In the future, I'll try to step away before I shout."
5. **Ask for Their Response**: Let them express how they felt. Listen without defensiveness.

If you do this promptly, you can sometimes repair the damage. Over time, consistent apologies plus changed behavior show that you are serious about handling anger better.

## 17. Professional Help for Chronic Anger

For some individuals, anger is not an occasional event but a frequent, intense problem. This might lead to repeated fights, damaged relationships, or even legal troubles. If you see signs of uncontrollable or extreme anger, seeking professional help is wise:

- **Therapists or Counselors**: They can identify triggers, teach coping methods, and guide you through underlying issues.
- **Anger Management Programs**: Structured courses often include group sessions where you learn and practice new skills.
- **Support Groups**: Sharing stories with others facing similar struggles can reduce shame and provide moral support.
- **Medical Evaluation**: Sometimes, mood disorders or other health conditions contribute to difficulty controlling anger.

Admitting you need help is not a weakness. It is a step toward a calmer, safer life.

---

## 18. When Someone Weaponizes Your Anger

Unfortunately, some people try to provoke you on purpose, hoping you will lose control so they can paint you as the "bad guy." If you sense someone is trying to push your buttons:

- **Recognize the Pattern**: They might bring up topics that they know make you angry in public or at critical moments.
- **Refuse to Engage**: Stay calm, use short answers, and do not let them drag you into a heated argument.
- **Document Their Behavior**: If it is happening at work or school, keep notes in case you need to report harassment.
- **Set Firm Boundaries**: If they do not stop, limit contact or involve an authority figure if necessary.
- **Keep Your Composure**: The calmer you remain, the less they can use your anger against you.

By being mindful, you can avoid falling into a trap that someone sets to make you explode in front of others.

## 19. Using Compassion Alongside Anger

Sometimes we feel angry at someone who is also suffering. For instance, a family member struggling with addiction might fail to keep promises, which enrages you. But you know they are not doing it just to hurt you.

- **Distinguish Problem from Person**: Their behavior is frustrating, but the person themselves might be battling a tough challenge.
- **Express Anger at the Actions**: "I'm furious that you took money from my room," while still recognizing they might need professional help.
- **Set Boundaries Wisely**: Compassion does not mean letting them repeat harmful acts. You might need to lock your belongings or seek outside assistance for them.
- **Encourage Help**: If possible, support them in finding solutions.
- **Care for Your Emotions**: Dealing with complicated anger and compassion can be draining. Seek your own support from friends or counselors.

Recognizing someone's struggle can temper raw anger and lead to a response that is both firm and caring.

# Chapter 15: Self-Control Steps

Self-control is the ability to manage your actions, feelings, and desires in a way that aligns with your values and goals. It keeps you from reacting automatically when something upsets you and allows you to think clearly about how you want to behave. When you have good self-control, you can pause before saying hurtful words, stop yourself from acting on impulses, and choose helpful responses in conflicts. Instead of letting anger or temptation decide your actions, you stay in charge.

In this chapter, we will look at why self-control matters, how it helps in various parts of life, and what steps you can use to build and strengthen it. We will also consider how self-control supports healthier relationships, clearer thinking, and calmer conflict resolution. By the end, you will have practical approaches for keeping a steady mind, even when situations stir strong emotions or test your patience.

---

## 1. What Is Self-Control?

Self-control involves pausing and reflecting before acting on a strong urge. This might be an urge to lash out when someone offends you, or an urge to eat something unhealthy when you are trying to stick to a plan. It does not mean ignoring your feelings; instead, it means allowing yourself time to understand and respond wisely. People who have strong self-control can sense a powerful emotion but still pick a response that fits their long-term goals, rather than just reacting in the heat of the moment.

**Self-Control vs. Suppression**

- **Self-control**: You acknowledge what you feel (anger, frustration, excitement) and gently guide your next steps.
- **Suppression**: You try to push down or ignore your emotions completely, pretending they are not there.

Suppression can lead to bigger explosions of emotion later because bottled-up feelings often come back stronger. Self-control is not about ignoring feelings; it is about handling them in a responsible way.

## 2. Why Is Self-Control Important?

Self-control benefits almost every area of life, from personal relationships to academic or career success:

- **Better Conflict Outcomes**: If you maintain control during a disagreement, you are more likely to resolve it peacefully. Instead of shouting or insulting the other person, you can discuss concerns calmly.
- **Stronger Relationships**: People trust and respect those who show composure. They know you will not lash out unexpectedly.
- **Improved Focus**: When you control impulses, you can pay attention to tasks without getting distracted by random urges or shifting moods.
- **Healthier Habits**: Self-control helps you follow through on plans such as exercise routines, balanced eating, or adequate rest.
- **Less Regret**: Acting on an impulse can lead to choices you regret soon after. Self-control gives you time to rethink hasty decisions.

In conflicts, self-control often decides whether you make the situation better or worse. A small moment of pause before reacting can keep a minor clash from growing into a large fight.

---

## 3. The Brain and Self-Control

Part of self-control happens in the front part of the brain, known as the prefrontal cortex. This region helps with planning, decision-making, and controlling impulses. When emotions like anger or excitement spike, parts of the brain that handle strong feelings (often in deeper regions) can override rational thought unless the prefrontal cortex steps in. This is why it can feel so hard to think straight in moments of intense emotion.

### Factors That Affect the Brain's Ability to Use Self-Control

- **Stress**: High stress can weaken the prefrontal cortex's ability to manage impulses.
- **Fatigue**: Being very tired reduces mental energy, making it harder to pause before acting.
- **Substances**: Alcohol or certain substances can lower inhibitions, leading to reduced self-control.

- **Hunger**: Low blood sugar or hunger can make people more irritable and less able to restrain themselves.

Knowing these factors helps you plan. For example, if you often argue with someone late at night when you are tired, you could try talking earlier in the day.

## 4. Recognizing Your Own Triggers

A big part of self-control is knowing what situations make it hardest for you to stay calm. Different people have different triggers, such as:

- **Being Teased**: Some people immediately flare up when teased or mocked.
- **Waiting**: Having to wait in a long line or for someone who is late might set off frustration.
- **Criticism**: Even gentle feedback can feel like an attack if you are sensitive in that area.
- **Stressful Environments**: Loud or chaotic places can overload your senses, making small annoyances bigger.
- **Certain Topics**: Discussions about money, politics, or past issues can spark strong emotions.

If you notice you always feel close to snapping in these scenarios, you can prepare in advance. For instance, remind yourself to breathe slowly if you know a meeting might include criticism, or limit your time in environments that push you over the edge.

## 5. The Pause: Your First Self-Control Step

When you sense a strong emotion rising, the first and most crucial step is to **pause**. A short pause (sometimes just a few seconds) creates a gap between your emotion and your action. During this gap, you can evaluate: "Is what I am about to do helpful or harmful?"

**Practical Ways to Pause**

- **Take a Deep Breath**: Inhale, hold it for a moment, and exhale slowly. This short action can interrupt the rush of anger or fear.

- **Count Silently**: Count up to three or five in your head before speaking.
- **Sip Water**: If possible, take a small sip of water. This simple act forces a short break and can ground you physically.
- **Look Away Briefly**: Shifting your gaze to something neutral (like a wall or a table) for a moment can reduce the intensity of eye-to-eye confrontation.

These might seem like small actions, but they can keep you from blurting out something harsh or doing something you will regret.

---

## 6. Setting Clear Goals for Your Behavior

Self-control improves when you have a clear idea of how you want to behave, even in stressful moments. For example, if your goal is to handle disagreements politely, remind yourself of that goal before a challenging talk. By having a set standard—"I will not raise my voice or insult them"—you create a guideline that can help you resist impulsive outbursts.

**Types of Behavior Goals**

- **Tone of Voice**: Decide that you will speak in a steady tone, not a yelling one.
- **Respectful Words**: Plan to avoid name-calling, cursing, or belittling language.
- **Listening Fully**: Commit to hearing the other side without interrupting, even if you disagree.
- **Timing**: If you know certain times are bad (e.g., when you are sleepy or hungry), you set a goal not to address big issues at those times.

When a heated situation arises, you can recall your goals. This mental reminder helps you steer your actions in line with those intentions.

---

## 7. Practicing Self-Control in Low-Stress Scenarios

It is wise to build your self-control muscle in smaller, everyday ways, rather than waiting for a huge conflict to test you:

- **Delay Small Pleasures**: If you want a snack, wait five minutes before getting it. This trains you to handle urges.
- **Manage Mild Frustrations**: If you are stuck in traffic, use that time to practice calm breathing instead of honking or ruminating.
- **Hold Off on Replies**: When you receive a message that annoys you, wait a short time before responding.
- **Stay Polite When Slightly Upset**: If a cashier is slow, or a friend is late, use it as a mini-challenge: "I will keep my composure."

These small exercises strengthen your ability to pause and reflect, making it more natural to do so during bigger conflicts.

---

## 8. Techniques for Sustaining Self-Control in Conflict

In a real disagreement, self-control has to last longer than a few seconds. Here are extended strategies:

### a) Use a Calm Anchor

Pick something in your surroundings—a piece of furniture, a pen in your hand, or the ground beneath your feet—and focus on it whenever anger bubbles up. This anchor reminds you to stay present and helps break the cycle of angry thoughts.

### b) Slow Down the Conversation

If the argument is getting heated, speak more slowly than normal. Pause before each sentence. This slower pace forces you to choose words carefully and reduces the chance of blurting out insults.

### c) Suggest a Brief Break

If you feel anger boiling, politely say, "I need a moment to think. Can we pause for a minute?" This is not running away; it is a step to ensure the conflict does not escalate. Agree to return and continue talking once you have cooled off.

### d) Check Feelings Regularly

Ask yourself, "Am I still calm enough to talk, or am I about to explode?" If the latter, use a break or a self-soothing method like quietly counting or focusing on breathing.

## 9. Handling Long-Lasting Disputes with Self-Control

Some disagreements do not end quickly; they might stretch over days or weeks. Keeping self-control in such prolonged conflicts takes extra care:

- **Plan Your Interactions**: Decide ahead of time when and how you will talk. For instance, if you are more composed in the morning, do not wait until late at night to have a serious discussion.
- **Set Boundaries**: If the other person triggers you often, limit the duration or frequency of interactions until you both can talk more calmly.
- **Seek Third-Party Help**: In an ongoing conflict, a mediator or counselor can guide talks and help you stick to respectful communication.
- **Use Written Communication**: If face-to-face talks spiral out of control, consider carefully worded letters or emails. This gives you time to craft a measured response.

Long disputes often bring repeated frustrations, so you need repeated reminders of your self-control plan. Keep track of your emotional energy and take breaks as needed.

---

## 10. The Role of Positive Habits in Self-Control

Strong self-control does not appear overnight; it grows from daily routines that support stability and clarity of mind:

- **Regular Exercise**: Even walking or light stretching can lower stress hormones, making it easier to stay calm under pressure.
- **Balanced Diet**: Sugary snacks might give quick bursts of energy but can lead to crashes, which can worsen mood swings.
- **Good Sleep**: A well-rested mind is more alert and better at resisting impulsive behavior.
- **Mindfulness Practice**: Short sessions of silent focus, paying attention to your breathing or body sensations, can sharpen your ability to notice and manage emotions.
- **Time Management**: Rushing and feeling behind schedule add stress. Organizing your tasks can reduce panic, leaving more mental resources for self-control.

When these habits are in place, you are less likely to be overwhelmed by minor triggers, because your body and mind are in a more balanced state.

---

## 11. Self-Control and Emotional Intelligence

Self-control is part of a bigger skill set called **emotional intelligence** (EI), which involves being aware of your feelings, guiding them in a helpful way, understanding others' emotions, and managing social interactions smoothly.

- **Awareness**: Notice your changing moods. "I feel tension in my shoulders. I am upset right now."
- **Regulation**: Decide how to handle that mood. "I need a moment to breathe so I do not lash out."
- **Empathy**: Recognize the other person also has strong feelings.
- **Social Skills**: Use respectful words, active listening, and compromise to keep the relationship healthy.

People with high EI typically show more self-control because they see the bigger picture of how each interaction affects relationships.

---

## 12. Teaching Self-Control to Younger Ones

Parents and caregivers can help children develop self-control early. Some ideas:

- **Create Clear Rules**: Let children know what behavior is acceptable. This clarity helps them understand when to pause.
- **Role-Play Scenarios**: Practice small conflicts in a safe setting, showing them how to remain calm.
- **Use Rewards Wisely**: Encourage them when they manage frustration or wait their turn. This supports their self-control attempts.
- **Calm Down Spots**: A quiet corner or comfy chair where they can go to self-soothe before returning to the group.
- **Lead by Example**: If parents shout at each other, kids learn to do the same. Demonstrating calm interactions teaches them best.

Starting young is powerful because repeated lessons mold their default reactions to stress or disagreement.

## 13. The Limits of Self-Control

While self-control is very useful, it is not a magic fix for every problem. Sometimes:

- **Problems Are External**: Even if you stay calm, the other side may be unreasonable or circumstances might be out of your hands.
- **You May Need Help**: If your anger stems from deep trauma or mental health conditions, professional help is important.
- **Temporarily Low Willpower**: Life events—like grief, major illness, or big stress—can sap your capacity for self-restraint, making you more prone to snapping.
- **Some Boundaries Must Be Enforced**: Self-control does not mean you must stay in harmful environments. In severe cases, leaving might be the best action.

Self-control is a powerful tool, but it is part of a larger toolkit that includes problem-solving, boundary-setting, and seeking assistance when needed.

---

## 14. Self-Control and Digital Spaces

Modern technology can challenge self-control. Quick access to social media or messaging can intensify conflicts if you respond instantly in anger. Some tips:

- **Pause Before Posting**: If you read something that makes you mad, wait a few minutes before replying.
- **Limit Notifications**: Fewer alerts can mean fewer sudden emotional reactions.
- **Draft and Review**: Write your message, then review it before hitting send. Are your words respectful and clear?
- **Manage Screen Time**: Endless scrolling can increase stress, making self-control weaker. Take breaks if you feel your emotions rising.
- **Log Out if Overwhelmed**: If an online argument heats up, step away to calm down instead of fueling it further.

Staying mindful of how quickly online exchanges can escalate is vital for maintaining self-control in the digital world.

## 15. Group Support for Self-Control

Sometimes, practicing self-control is easier with support. You could:

- **Form a Small Accountability Group**: A few friends agree to help each other remain calm under stress. If you feel yourself getting close to losing control, you can message them for encouragement.
- **Join a Class or Workshop**: Some community centers offer sessions on stress management or mindful communication, giving you new strategies.
- **Talk with Trusted Mentors**: A teacher, coach, or community leader might share tips on staying poised during tough times.

Having people who understand your struggles and cheer you on can boost your motivation to keep practicing self-control.

## 16. Self-Control for Long-Term Goals

Self-control is not only about handling anger or short-term urges. It also fuels your ability to stick to longer-term aims:

- **Academic or Career Goals**: Requires consistent effort, ignoring distractions. Self-control helps you do the tasks when you do not feel like it.
- **Financial Goals**: Sticking to a budget, saving money, or avoiding impulsive purchases.
- **Health Goals**: Following through on exercise routines or staying away from unhealthy habits.
- **Personal Projects**: Maybe writing a book, learning an instrument, or working on a hobby. Self-control ensures you keep going when the excitement fades.

Each time you resist a short-term urge in favor of a long-term benefit, you strengthen self-control, which also applies to conflict situations. The discipline to avoid yelling at someone in frustration is connected to the discipline to keep practicing a skill even when it is hard.

## 17. Signs You Are Improving Self-Control

Over time, you might notice:

1. **Less Reactivity**: Situations that once made you blow up might now only mildly irritate you.
2. **Quicker Recovery**: Even if you get upset, you calm down faster and do not dwell on it.
3. **Better Outcomes**: You might see fewer fights, more friendly talks, and stronger bonds with friends or family.
4. **Improved Confidence**: You trust yourself to handle challenges without losing control.
5. **Reduced Regret**: You do not keep replaying embarrassing or harmful moments of anger in your mind.

These changes might be small at first, but every step forward is progress.

---

## 18. Self-Reflection and Monitoring

A good habit is to reflect after each conflict or challenging situation:

- **What Triggered Me?** Identify what set off the anger or impulse.
- **Did I Pause?** If you did, how did that help? If you did not, why not?
- **How Did I Respond?** Did you follow your self-control plan or slip into old habits?
- **What Could I Do Better Next Time?** Think of at least one change to make in future.
- **Any Positive Takeaway?** Even if it was tough, maybe you managed not to shout, or you ended the talk more peacefully than before.

Regular self-checks turn everyday situations into learning experiences, helping you fine-tune your self-control.

# Chapter 16: Calming Down in Tense Times

Staying calm when tensions rise can feel difficult. Stressful moments might trigger anger, worry, or strong frustration, causing us to act in ways we later regret. Yet staying calm is essential for clear thinking, effective communication, and peaceful resolutions. When you can calm yourself, you avoid making conflicts bigger than they need to be. You can also help others relax, because calmness often spreads. This chapter will look at why it is so hard to stay calm in tense situations, then offer practical methods to steady your emotions. By learning to soothe your body and mind, you build a foundation for healthier relationships and more successful conflict resolution.

---

### 1. Why Tension Makes Us Lose Calmness

Tension naturally activates our body's stress response, commonly known as the "fight or flight" reaction. This built-in survival system aims to protect us from threats. Imagine ancient times: if a person saw a wild animal, the body would release chemicals like adrenaline, getting muscles ready to run or fight. In modern life, strong tension can still trigger those same chemicals, even if the "danger" is just an argument or a challenging conversation rather than a physical threat.

- **Physical Alarm**: Heart rate speeds up, breathing becomes shallow, and muscles tighten.
- **Narrowed Thoughts**: We focus mostly on the perceived threat. We may ignore positive or calming details around us.
- **Heightened Emotions**: Anger or fear intensifies. Adrenaline and related hormones create a sense of urgency, like we must react now.

Although this system helps protect us when real danger exists, it can cause problems in normal conflicts. Instead of thinking logically, we might snap or yell, say hurtful things, or storm out. Recognizing that this reaction is part of our biology is the first step. Once we know tension triggers our body's alarm response, we can practice ways to quiet it.

## 2. The Cost of Not Calming Down

Sometimes we may think that showing how upset we are will force the other side to cooperate. Or we might believe letting out anger fully is the only way to get relief. But losing calmness usually carries big costs:

1. **Damaged Relationships**: Intense displays of anger—shouting, mocking, slamming doors—often scare or hurt others. They might pull away, losing trust in us.
2. **Poor Decision-Making**: When tension is high, logical thinking drops. We might accuse someone without evidence or demand unfair things.
3. **Lingering Stress**: After a heated reaction, we often feel guilty, embarrassed, or exhausted. The tension can remain in our body for hours or even days.
4. **Escalation of Conflict**: Once calmness is lost, each side may act more aggressively. The cycle of blame can spiral.
5. **Loss of Control**: We might say or do things that do not match our true values, leaving us to regret it later.

Calming down does not mean letting people walk over us. It means choosing not to let our alarm system drive the conversation. That choice leads to clearer minds, better solutions, and fewer regrets.

---

## 3. Physical Approaches to Calm the Body

One path to calmness is easing the physical side of tension. Since strong emotion affects your body, soothing physical tension can help quiet your mind.

### a) Deep, Slow Breathing

- **How**: Inhale through the nose for a slow count of four. Pause slightly. Exhale through the mouth for another slow count of four.
- **Why**: This tells your nervous system that the threat may be lower than it seems. It also interrupts shallow, rapid breathing that often accompanies stress.

### b) Progressive Muscle Relaxation

- **How**: Pick a muscle group (like your hands) and tighten those muscles for a few seconds, then release. Move through muscle groups—from arms to shoulders to legs.
- **Why**: Tightening and releasing helps you notice where tension is stored. As you let each group relax, your overall tension lowers.

### c) Guided Imagery

- **How**: Imagine a peaceful setting, such as a quiet beach or a calm forest. Picture details: the color of the sky, the sound of leaves, the feel of sand or grass.
- **Why**: The brain can react to imagined scenes in ways similar to real ones. Focusing on a calm place can reduce stress signals in your body.

### d) Calming Touch

- **How**: Place a hand on your chest or gently rub your arms. If you have a pet or a soft item near you, touching it can also help.
- **Why**: Gentle physical contact can release soothing chemicals in the body. This is why hugging a loved one can feel comforting.

These methods do not require special tools or much time, so you can use them discreetly in many situations—during a heated discussion at home, a tense team meeting, or even a quick break in a hallway.

---

## 4. Mental Techniques for Calmness

Calming the mind is just as important as calming the body. Negative or anxious thoughts often stoke the fires of tension, whereas balanced thinking cools them.

### a) Thought Check

When tension arises, certain thoughts might flood your mind:

- "They always do this to me!"
- "I cannot stand this anymore!"
- "I have to fight back or I'll lose!"

Ask yourself: **Is this thought accurate or is it an exaggeration?** Could the situation be more complex? Replacing "They always do this" with "They have done this a few times and it is upsetting, but maybe there is a reason or a misunderstanding" can help reduce the intensity.

**b) Positive Mental Reminders**

Think of short, calming phrases:

- "I can handle this."
- "Staying calm helps me see the best solution."
- "It's okay to step back and breathe."

These simple reminders counter frantic thoughts, grounding you in a calmer mindset.

**c) Visualize a Better Outcome**

Picture the conflict ending in a respectful conversation or a fair compromise. Even if it seems unlikely, imagining a better outcome can shift your approach. You might unconsciously start acting in ways that make that outcome more likely, rather than fueling a blow-up.

**d) Mindful Observation**

Focus on what your senses detect right now—the sounds in the background, any scents in the air, the texture of your clothing. This pulls your mind away from racing thoughts about the future or past and places it in the present moment, where you can manage your reactions more effectively.

---

## 5. Calming Strategies for Different Conflict Settings

Conflicts can arise in many places—home, school, work, or public spaces. Each environment might require a slightly different approach to calmness.

- **At Home**: You might step into another room for a quick breathing exercise if a conversation gets too heated. Because you have more privacy, you can do a short muscle relaxation sequence.

- **At Work**: You may not have the freedom to leave a meeting abruptly. Instead, practice subtle deep breathing, keep your posture upright, and perhaps ask for a brief break if possible.
- **At School**: If tension flares with classmates, you might use quiet self-talk or suggest talking to a teacher or counselor after a short pause.
- **Public Places**: If a stranger or situation escalates, focusing on your breathing or stepping away from the immediate area might be best. Avoid reacting impulsively in a crowd where safety could be a concern.

Tailor your calm-down plan to each setting's limitations. Knowing in advance how you will respond in each place can keep you steady.

## 6. The Power of Short Breaks

One of the most effective calm-down methods is simply stepping away for a moment. When tension peaks, staying face-to-face can keep adrenaline high. A short break disrupts the stress cycle.

- **How Long**: It can be as short as 30 seconds or as long as a few minutes. You might say, "I need a moment to think," or, "Let me grab a glass of water."
- **What to Do**: During that break, breathe deeply, stretch your legs, or repeat a calming phrase in your mind.
- **Agree to Return**: If you are in a serious discussion, reassure the other person you are not ignoring them. You will come back to finish talking once you have calmed down.

Taking a break is not the same as running away from the conflict. It is a tactical pause that prevents saying or doing things in anger. Returning with a clearer head helps the conversation stay more productive.

## 7. Listening as a Calming Tool

Oddly enough, one of the best ways to calm yourself is to focus on the other person's words. When tension rises, we tend to either talk over them or mentally prepare our next argument. But active listening can bring unexpected calmness:

1. **Focus on Their Feelings**: Try to figure out what they are experiencing, such as worry, anger, or sadness.
2. **Reflect Their Points**: Quietly paraphrase in your mind: "They feel left out because I did not tell them about my plans."
3. **Ask Clarifying Questions**: Gently ask, "Could you say more about what upset you?" This approach slows the pace of the conflict and can lower emotional volume.
4. **Delay Your Retorts**: Do not jump in with your defense right away. Let them finish. This waiting time helps your own tension drop as well.

Listening serves two goals: it helps you gather more facts and shows you are not just there to fight. In many disputes, once the other person sees you care enough to hear them, their anger or frustration may dial down too. This calmer back-and-forth sets the stage for a more thoughtful resolution.

---

## 8. Calming Others by Modeling Calmness

If you are calm, it can influence the people around you to calm down as well. Emotions are often contagious. Yelling can lead to more yelling, while a soft, steady tone can encourage quieter, more measured responses. This does not mean you must silently accept their anger. Rather, you show how to keep composure:

- **Body Language**: Keep your posture relaxed, hands unclenched, face neutral or gently concerned. Avoid rolling your eyes or smirking.
- **Voice Tone**: Speak a bit slower and quieter if they are getting loud. Do not match their volume.
- **Respectful Words**: Even if they accuse you unfairly, reply with courtesy. "I hear what you're saying, and I'd like to talk this through calmly."
- **Suggest Calm Action**: "Maybe we can both sit for a second, take a breath, and then keep talking."

By holding onto calmness, you become an anchor in the storm. You might not solve the conflict immediately, but you prevent it from turning into a full-blown fight and guide it toward a more reasoned dialogue.

---

## 9. Long-Term Benefits of Learning to Calm Down

Calming yourself is not just useful during arguments. Over time, it changes how you handle stress altogether:

1. **Reduced Stress Levels**: By not letting tension escalate constantly, your body and mind get fewer stress hormones. This can improve health.
2. **Enhanced Emotional Control**: Each time you practice calming, you strengthen neural pathways that help you stay balanced in future challenges.
3. **Better Problem-Solving**: A calmer approach keeps your mind open to new ideas and creative solutions.
4. **Positive Reputation**: People will see you as someone who handles tough situations gracefully, increasing trust and respect.
5. **Fewer Relationship Clashes**: It is easier to maintain healthy bonds when arguments do not spiral out of control.

Developing calmness is an investment in your overall well-being. It affects how you manage everything from minor disappointments to major life obstacles.

---

## 10. Children and Teens: Teaching Calmness Early

Parents and educators can help young people build calmness from a young age. This involves showing them step by step how to handle frustration or anger:

- **Explain Feelings**: Let kids know it is okay to feel upset, but they have choices about how to express it.
- **Simple Techniques**: Teach them to take a "balloon breath" (imagine inflating a balloon in their belly) or to close their eyes and count slowly.
- **Model Calmness**: If adults remain calm in a child's tantrum or meltdown, the child eventually learns from that example.
- **Praise Calm Efforts**: Acknowledge it when they use their calm-down skills, like stepping away instead of hitting or yelling.
- **Safe Calming Area**: Sometimes called a "quiet corner." The child can go there to cool off, with comforting items like pillows or a favorite book.

Establishing these habits early helps children enter adulthood with natural tools for staying steady in storms of emotion.

## 11. Warning Signs That Calming Methods Are Not Enough

While calming strategies help most common disputes, there are times when you need stronger actions:

1. **Threats or Violence**: If someone is physically aggressive or threatening serious harm, the focus must shift to safety. Calm words alone might not stop them. Seek help from authorities or find a safe escape.
2. **Deep Trauma**: If tensions trigger past trauma responses—extreme panic, flashbacks, or uncontrollable fear—professional therapy might be essential.
3. **Prolonged High-Stress Environment**: When you are stuck in a situation (like an abusive home or workplace) that never gives you a chance to recover, your body might remain in constant alert mode. In such cases, seeking outside support or changing environments is crucial.
4. **Recurring Harmful Patterns**: If, despite attempts to calm down, your conflicts always become hurtful, it may be time for family counseling or structured mediation.

Calmness techniques are powerful but do not replace needed safety steps or professional care if the situation is severe.

---

## 12. Calmness and Assertiveness

Staying calm does not mean being passive. You can be calm and still stand up for your rights or express strong opinions. This is known as **assertiveness**—firmly stating your views without shouting or attacking:

- **Calm Language**: "I disagree with your point, but I want to discuss it respectfully."
- **Clear Requests**: "Could we find a way to share the tasks more fairly?" instead of snapping, "You never do your part!"
- **Sticking to Key Issues**: Focus on what truly matters, not past grudges or personal attacks.
- **Flexibility**: Even while being firm, show willingness to hear new ideas.

Combining calmness with assertiveness allows you to maintain dignity and handle conflict effectively. You do not have to yield every point or hide your frustration; you simply channel it into a balanced conversation.

## 13. Techniques for Calming Anxiety in a Conflict

Sometimes, tension does not cause anger but anxiety—fear of confrontation, dread of hurting someone, or worry about the outcome.

- **Self-Reassurance**: Silently remind yourself, "I can handle discussing this. Even if it is uncomfortable, I will be okay."
- **Grounding Exercises**: Name five things you see around you, four things you can feel, three things you can hear, two you can smell, and one you can taste (if relevant). This root-in-the-present method often reduces anxiety spikes.
- **Plan Key Points**: If anxiety comes from not knowing what to say, outline two or three main points in advance. Then you are less likely to freeze.
- **Ask Questions**: Anxiety often grows from uncertainty. Request details: "Could you clarify what you mean by that?" Once things are clearer, your worry might lessen.
- **Gentle Visualization**: Picture yourself speaking calmly and the other person listening. Even if it does not go exactly that way, you have set a positive tone in your mind.

These steps help shift the mindset from fearful anticipation to manageable action, preserving calmness in the process.

---

## 14. Using Humor Carefully to Reduce Tension

In some cases, a bit of light humor can defuse tension. Humor should be used wisely and respectfully:

- **Gentle, Not Sarcastic**: Sarcasm can sound like an attack. Keep humor mild, maybe pointing to something neutral in the environment, not mocking the other person.
- **Never Laugh at Their Feelings**: If the other person is upset, do not joke about their distress. This can make them feel insulted.
- **Self-Irony**: A small, harmless joke about your own mistake can show humility, like "Wow, I sure chose the best day to forget my notes," if you are the one who messed up.

- **Check the Mood**: If the conflict is truly serious, humor might come across as insensitive. Use it only when tension is mild or if you see the other person is open to it.

When done right, a soft chuckle can momentarily break the storm's momentum, letting both sides breathe and reset. But if you sense the other person is too angry or hurt, it is better to rely on straightforward calming methods rather than jokes.

---

## 15. Group Calming in Meetings or Gatherings

Tense moments often appear in group settings—like committee meetings or family gatherings. Collective calmness can be cultivated by:

1. **Structured Speaking**: Each person gets a turn to share concerns without interruption. This slows the group's tempo and prevents chaotic shouting.
2. **Facilitator Role**: A moderator can gently remind people to keep voices down or try a brief stretch break if arguments heat up.
3. **Agreeing on Calm Rules**: Before diving into big topics, the group can decide, "No personal attacks," or "We can pause if someone needs a moment."
4. **Summaries and Clarifications**: Pausing regularly to summarize what has been said helps everyone process calmly rather than talk over one another.

When calmness becomes a group norm, people feel safer voicing ideas, and solutions tend to be more creative and fair.

---

## 16. Digital Conflicts: Calming Strategies Online

Online arguments can be surprisingly intense. The lack of face-to-face cues can increase misunderstandings and harsh words:

- **Pause Before Replying**: If an online comment makes you angry, wait. Give yourself at least a few minutes, or even a day, to cool off.

- **Draft Your Reply**: Type it in a separate place, then read it again later. Often, you will decide to soften or shorten it.
- **Use Emojis or Clear Language**: Sometimes, a simple respectful word or a mild emoji can convey tone. But avoid sarcasm that can be misread.
- **Move to a Private Channel**: If a group chat flares up, invite the other person to talk in direct messages or a private call to avoid a public showdown.
- **Know When to Log Off**: Some disagreements do not resolve easily online. If your emotions keep rising, close the app or site and return after you have calmed.

Digital calmness requires conscious effort, because written text lacks the softening effect of eye contact or voice tone. The self-discipline to slow down or step away is crucial.

---

## 17. Combining Calmness with Problem-Solving

Calming down is not the final goal; it is a tool to help you solve the actual conflict. Once both sides are calmer, real problem-solving can begin:

- **Define the Issue**: With steady minds, you can pinpoint what the disagreement is truly about.
- **Gather Facts**: Emotions no longer cloud your view, so you can check details or data more objectively.
- **Brainstorm Solutions**: Calmness fosters creativity. You might see compromise options you missed before.
- **Mutual Respect**: When everyone is calmer, each side is more likely to respect the other's needs.
- **Set Next Steps**: Wrap up with clear decisions or agreements. If new tension arises, you can calm down again and continue.

Remember, calmness does not solve everything alone, but it paves the way for a constructive resolution process.

---

## 18. Avoiding "False Calmness"

Sometimes people appear calm on the outside but seethe with anger or resentment inside. They might hold back words to keep the peace short term, yet their anger does not truly subside. This can lead to sudden blow-ups later or passive-aggressive behavior. True calmness involves:

- **Acknowledging Emotions**: You notice your upset feelings but work to cool them, not pretend they do not exist.
- **Breathing or Soothing Tools**: Instead of swallowing anger, you use real methods to reduce it.
- **Respectful Expression**: Once calmer, you address the problem in words, stating your feelings and concerns.
- **Seeking Resolution**: You do not bury the problem forever. Calmness is meant to help you talk about it in a balanced way, not ignore it.

If you sense you are faking calm, take extra steps—like journaling or seeking a friend's advice—to process the deeper frustration. Keeping the conflict hidden can lead to bigger trouble down the line.

---

## 19. Tracking Your Progress

Building the habit of calmness takes time. Tracking small improvements can encourage you to keep going:

- **Keep a Journal**: Note each time you manage to stay calm under pressure. Write what worked and how you felt afterward.
- **Use a Rating Scale**: After each conflict, rate your calmness from 1 to 10. Over weeks or months, see if your scores improve.
- **Celebrate Small Wins**: If you avoided yelling or overcame an impulse, mentally acknowledge that success.
- **Learn from Slips**: If you lost your cool, do not be harsh on yourself. Instead, reflect on what triggered you, so you are better prepared next time.

These steps keep you aware that calmness is a skill you are growing. In time, you might be pleasantly surprised by how often you remain composed in tense situations.

# Chapter 17: Asking for Support

Sometimes, conflict becomes too big, confusing, or painful to handle on our own. We might try to stay calm, practice self-control, or use respectful communication, yet the problem feels unsolvable by our efforts alone. In these moments, seeking outside help or leaning on supportive people can make all the difference. Whether we talk to trusted friends, family members, counselors, or professional mediators, we gain fresh perspectives and emotional backup. We also tap into resources that we might not have as individuals. Asking for support is not a sign of weakness; it is a smart step that often leads to better solutions and prevents conflicts from growing worse.

In this chapter, we will discuss reasons for seeking help, the types of support available, and how to approach others when you need assistance. We will also explore how to stay open to their advice without giving up your own voice in the conflict. By understanding the role of outside support, you can handle tough disagreements more calmly, knowing you do not have to face everything alone.

---

## 1. Why Seek Support?

Many people are hesitant to ask for help, worrying they might seem incapable or that they will burden someone else. However, support can be crucial because:

1. **Complex Conflicts**: Some disagreements involve many layers—emotions, finances, personal history, or misunderstandings. Outside help can clarify these layers.
2. **High Emotions**: When anger or fear is too strong, it is hard to see all angles. Another person's calm view can keep things balanced.
3. **Power Differences**: If one side holds more power (like a boss or older family member), a neutral third party can ensure fairness.
4. **Emotional Strain**: Prolonged conflict can lead to stress, anxiety, or hopelessness. Support from friends or counselors offers emotional relief.
5. **Fresh Ideas**: Someone not directly involved might suggest solutions you never considered. They bring an outside perspective that can cut through the tension.

Asking for support is often the difference between a conflict that drags on painfully and one that finds resolution or at least better understanding.

## 2. Identifying the Kind of Support You Need

Not all conflicts are alike, so the type of help you seek can differ. Some common forms of support include:

- **Emotional Support**: A friend who listens, a family member who offers comfort, or a support group that understands your situation. Emotional support gives you a safe space to vent, process feelings, and reduce stress.
- **Practical Help**: People who can offer direct assistance, like helping you gather documents for a conflict at work or standing beside you as you address a school issue.
- **Advice or Guidance**: Mentors, older relatives, or teachers who have dealt with similar problems. They can share lessons learned or point you toward resources.
- **Professional Mediation**: Neutral professionals trained to help conflicting parties communicate and find common ground.
- **Legal or Official Assistance**: Lawyers, union representatives, or advocates who protect your rights in serious disputes (for example, workplace harassment or custody issues).
- **Counseling or Therapy**: A mental health professional who helps you navigate complex emotions, trauma, or patterns of conflict in relationships.

Figuring out which area you need help in clarifies who you should approach. Sometimes you need a combination—like emotional support from friends plus professional advice from a counselor.

## 3. Choosing the Right Person or Resource

After you decide what type of help you need, it is time to pick whom to ask. Consider:

1. **Trustworthiness**: Do you trust them to keep private things confidential if needed?
2. **Relevant Experience**: Have they successfully navigated similar conflicts or do they have professional expertise?
3. **Availability**: Are they able and willing to give the time and attention your conflict needs?
4. **Neutrality**: If you need a mediator, pick someone who is neutral, not heavily biased toward one side.
5. **Comfort Level**: You must feel comfortable opening up, or else you may hold back important details.

In some cases, you might talk to more than one person, like confiding in a friend for emotional support but also consulting a specialized mediator if the conflict is complicated.

---

## 4. How to Ask for Support

Asking for support can feel awkward if you are not used to it. A few pointers can help:

1. **Be Honest and Clear**: Explain the situation briefly and why you need help. For instance, "I'm having a hard time at work with my supervisor, and I could use your advice on how to handle it."
2. **State What You Hope For**: Are you seeking emotional comfort, practical suggestions, or an active mediator role? Let them know.
3. **Respect Their Limits**: They might have limited time or expertise. If they cannot offer the help you want, do not take it personally. Ask if they can suggest someone else.
4. **Provide Background**: If the conflict is complex, share the main points so they understand the context. But try not to overwhelm them with every detail right away.
5. **Stay Open**: Allow them to ask questions or request clarification. This helps them offer the best support possible.

Keep the request direct but polite. Most people appreciate being asked for help, as it shows trust and respect for their input.

## 5. The Role of Friends and Family

Friends and family are often the first people we turn to when conflict becomes stressful. They can offer emotional backing, share relevant experiences, or just be a listening ear. However, there are some caution points:

- **Possible Bias**: Friends or relatives might side with you without hearing the other side, which can feed your anger or negativity instead of helping you see the full picture.
- **Risk of Gossip**: If a relative cannot keep things private, your conflict details might spread, causing more trouble.
- **Unwanted Judgment**: Some loved ones might become too involved, telling you what to do without truly listening.
- **Varied Advice Quality**: While they may mean well, not everyone has good conflict resolution skills. They might suggest approaches that worsen the issue.

To manage these risks, pick friends or family members who are calm, respectful, and known for giving balanced input. Make it clear you value their thoughts but want them to be honest rather than just taking your side automatically.

---

## 6. Support from Teachers or Coaches (for Students and Young People)

Young people in school or sports might find guidance from teachers, coaches, or school counselors:

- **Teachers**: They often have a broader view of classroom or peer conflicts. If you and a classmate constantly clash, a teacher can mediate or suggest ways to handle it.
- **Counselors**: Many schools have counselors trained to help students manage stress, bullying, or family issues. They keep conversations private unless there is a serious safety concern.
- **Coaches**: In sports teams, coaches can notice conflicts among teammates. Approaching them can lead to fairer rules or new ways to foster team harmony.

Adults in these roles typically want to help you succeed in a healthy environment. If you are too nervous to approach them in public, ask for a quick private chat or send them a note or email if your school allows it.

## 7. When Professional Mediation Is Helpful

Professional mediators specialize in conflict resolution. They do not take sides. Instead, they guide both parties to communicate better and explore solutions. This can be especially helpful in:

1. **Workplace Disputes**: Between employees or between management and staff, where tensions can be high and job security is on the line.
2. **Family Conflicts**: Divorce settlements, custody issues, or major family disagreements.
3. **Community or Neighbor Disputes**: Property lines, noise complaints, or other ongoing problems that normal communication fails to solve.
4. **Legal Conflicts**: Court systems sometimes encourage or require mediation before a trial, to reduce costs and find amicable solutions.

Mediators are trained in neutral listening, reframing harsh language, and helping both sides find common ground. They keep the process structured, ensuring each person gets to speak and no one dominates through loudness or intimidation.

---

## 8. Therapy and Counseling for Deep-Rooted Issues

Some conflicts arise from deeper emotional or psychological patterns—such as unresolved childhood experiences, trauma, or long-term relationship problems. In these cases, a counselor or therapist can help:

- **Identify Root Causes**: They can uncover why certain triggers bring out intense anger or fear.
- **Teach Coping Strategies**: Therapists often provide techniques for self-soothing, better communication, and emotional control.
- **Guide Relationship Therapy**: Family or couples therapy can help members talk in a safe, structured setting, improving trust and empathy.
- **Address Mental Health Concerns**: Anxiety, depression, or post-traumatic stress can increase conflict. Treating these issues may reduce tension significantly.

While therapy may seem like a big step, it can bring lasting benefits. If you see the same harmful patterns repeating in your life, or if conflicts cause severe distress, a mental health professional's support can be life-changing.

## 9. Using Online Support or Hotlines

In our digital age, numerous helplines, chat services, and online communities offer assistance. These can be anonymous and convenient:

- **Hotlines**: Many places have 24-hour hotlines or text lines for people in crisis. If a conflict triggers extreme anxiety or fear, a phone call can help you calm down and plan next steps.
- **Online Forums**: Some forums or social media groups discuss conflict resolution or specific types of disputes (like co-parenting or workplace issues). Be careful about oversharing personal data online, though.
- **Video Counseling**: Virtual therapy sessions let you talk to a licensed counselor from home. This is especially useful if you cannot find a local therapist.
- **Support Groups**: These can be for anything from relationship struggles to living with someone who has anger issues. Shared experiences help you feel less alone and gain fresh ideas.

Always check the credibility of online sources. While many are genuine, some might spread misinformation or be biased. Look for professional credentials or official hotline endorsements.

---

## 10. How to Prepare Before Getting Support

When you decide to seek help, some preparation can make the conversation smoother:

1. **Organize Facts**: Write down key points of the conflict—dates, main disagreements, attempts to fix the problem so far.
2. **Reflect on Your Role**: Be ready to explain not just what the other person did, but also how you may have contributed. People can help better if you are honest about your own part.
3. **List Your Questions**: Think about what exactly you want from this helper. Do you need strategies for calmness, or do you want them to intervene directly?
4. **Consider Possible Outcomes**: Are you hoping for a quick fix or a longer discussion process? Knowing your hopes can guide the support person's approach.

5. **Stay Open**: Be prepared to hear suggestions you have not considered. It might feel uncomfortable, but fresh perspectives often spark new solutions.

This preparation shows you are serious and respectful of the support person's time. It also makes it easier for them to grasp the situation quickly.

---

## 11. Communicating Clearly During Support

Once you have the helper's time, ensure you use it effectively:

- **Tell the Story Calmly**: Try not to vent in a chaotic way. Organize your account: what happened, why it matters, and how you feel.
- **Include Relevant Details**: Provide context but do not overload them with every tiny event—focus on key facts and examples.
- **Stay Balanced**: If you blame the other person entirely, the helper might doubt your objectivity. Acknowledge any points where you might have made mistakes or misunderstandings.
- **Ask for Their View**: Let them share their thoughts and ask clarifying questions.
- **Take Notes**: Jot down key advice or steps suggested. Emotions might make you forget them otherwise.

Being truthful and organized helps the support person give the best help. If they sense you are leaving out information or exaggerating, they may not be able to guide you properly.

---

## 12. Accepting Advice vs. Keeping Your Autonomy

When you ask for support, you might receive lots of advice. Some might be excellent; other suggestions may not fit your situation. How do you handle it?

1. **Listen Fully**: Even if you disagree at first, hear them out. They might have insights you have not considered.
2. **Ask for Reasons**: "Why do you think that approach would help?" Understanding their logic can clarify if it truly applies to your conflict.

3. **Evaluate Carefully**: Does the advice align with your values and goals? Could it harm anyone involved? Is it realistic in your setting?
4. **Stay True to Yourself**: In the end, you decide what to do. The supporter's role is to guide, not command.
5. **Combine Ideas**: You can adapt their suggestions. If they propose a big step you are not ready for, maybe you tweak it into a smaller first step.

Preserving your autonomy does not mean ignoring advice. It means applying what works best for you while respecting the helper's effort.

---

## 13. Emotional Boundaries When Seeking Help

Sometimes, you might lean heavily on one person for support, sharing every detail or repeatedly venting about the same conflict. This can strain the relationship if you do not recognize their limits:

- **Watch for Burnout**: If they start avoiding you or seem impatient, they might feel overwhelmed.
- **Vary Your Support Sources**: Rely on more than one person or group, so no single helper feels overloaded.
- **Appreciate Their Time**: A quick thank-you note or verbal gratitude can mean a lot.
- **Respect Their Advice**: Even if you do not follow it exactly, treat it with consideration.
- **Give Updates**: If someone gave you guidance, let them know briefly how it turned out. This closes the loop and shows respect for their involvement.

Healthy support involves mutual respect. You share your struggles and let them help, but you also stay mindful of their well-being.

---

## 14. Supporting Someone Who Supports You

When people help you, consider how you can maintain a caring relationship with them:

1. **Offer Support in Return**: Show interest in their life too. Let them know you are ready to listen if they ever face issues.
2. **Check In**: A simple "How are you feeling?" can go a long way, reminding them you value them as a person, not just as a problem-solver.
3. **Celebrate Their Effort**: Kindly acknowledge that they took time or emotional energy to help you. You might say, "I really appreciate you spending time to talk through this with me."
4. **Avoid Taking Advantage**: Do not treat them like an on-call helper. Recognize they have boundaries, schedules, and stress of their own.
5. **Learn and Apply**: Show that their help makes a difference. If they gave you conflict resolution tips, try them. Let them see you are serious about improving the situation.

Making sure your helper feels valued encourages them to continue supporting you if new conflicts emerge. It also preserves the friendship or relationship from one-sided strain.

## 15. Cultural Differences in Seeking Support

In some cultures, it is common to involve community members or elders in personal conflicts. In others, people might prefer to keep problems private. If you come from a background where seeking help is discouraged, you might feel uneasy about it. Conversely, if your culture emphasizes collective problem-solving, you might quickly gather the family to discuss an issue. Whichever approach you are used to:

- **Acknowledge Cultural Norms**: Understand how your cultural background influences your view of asking for help.
- **Balance Privacy and Openness**: Sometimes you can share just enough details for assistance without revealing every personal aspect of your life.
- **Explore Local Resources**: Some communities have elder councils or religious leaders who mediate disputes in a way that fits cultural values.
- **Stay True to Your Comfort Level**: If you prefer more privacy, pick a helper who respects confidentiality. If you like group involvement, ensure it is done in a respectful manner.

Cultural awareness can make the support process feel more natural and less stressful.

## 16. Handling Fear of Judgment

One big barrier to seeking support is the fear that others will judge or blame us. This fear is understandable, but remember:

- **Supporters Usually Want to Help**: People who offer help—counselors, friends, or mediators—know that everyone faces conflicts. They do not see you as "weak."
- **Confidentiality Rules**: Professionals like therapists, lawyers, or certain mediators have confidentiality guidelines. They cannot share your information without your permission (except in extreme cases like threats of harm).
- **Shared Humanity**: We all have disagreements or emotional struggles. The person you fear might judge you probably went through their own conflicts at some point.
- **Focus on Growth**: If you keep silent to avoid judgment, the conflict might remain unsolved. Seeking help could lead to a real solution and personal growth.

Overcoming the worry of being judged is part of building courage and self-care. Often, you will discover that genuine helpers show compassion rather than criticism.

---

## 17. Technology Tools for Organized Conflict Resolution

Beyond direct human support, there are also digital tools that can help:

- **Conflict Resolution Apps**: Some apps guide you through steps to clarify issues, set ground rules, and propose solutions.
- **Shared Calendars/Task Lists**: For household or workplace conflicts about chores or tasks, using a shared digital list can reduce confusion and friction.
- **Communication Platforms**: If meeting in person is hard, video calls or group chat software might allow a neutral facilitator to join from afar.
- **Online Mediation Services**: Certain sites offer formal mediation sessions through video conference. This can be useful when parties live far apart.

These tools complement personal help from friends or professionals. They organize the conflict resolution process and keep track of agreements.

## 18. Knowing When to End a Help-Seeking Relationship

Sometimes, the support you receive stops being helpful or runs its course:

- **The Conflict Is Resolved**: If you have found a solution or moved on, you may not need continued sessions or advice.
- **Mismatch in Approaches**: If a helper pushes methods that clash strongly with your values or repeatedly misjudges the situation, it might be time to seek different guidance.
- **Increased Tension**: If you sense the helper is causing more conflict—maybe they gossip about your situation or add personal bias—it is better to step away.
- **Lifestyle Changes**: You might move or your schedule might shift, making regular meetings impossible.

Ending a help relationship politely means thanking them for their time and letting them know you are ready to handle things independently or with a different form of support. If your conflict resurfaces, you can reconnect or find another resource.

---

## 19. Offering Support to Others in Conflict

Just as you can seek help, you might also be the helper for someone else. Key tips for offering support effectively:

1. **Listen with Empathy**: Let them share their story without jumping in too soon with solutions.
2. **Respect Their Feelings**: Acknowledge their emotions are real, even if you might see the situation differently.
3. **Ask What They Need**: Maybe they want just a listener or they are seeking advice. Let them lead.
4. **Stay Neutral When Possible**: If they ask you to mediate, try not to pick sides unless you see clear harm being done.
5. **Suggest Professional Help**: If the conflict is severe, encourage them to talk to a counselor, mediator, or someone with the right expertise.

Supporting someone else can also teach you about your own conflict style. You might see behaviors in them that mirror your own and realize how to improve.

# Chapter 18: Positive Change from Conflict

Many people see conflict as only a negative force—something to avoid or end as quickly as possible. While it is true that conflict can bring discomfort and stress, it can also lead to progress. In fact, many important breakthroughs in families, schools, workplaces, and communities happen because of conflicts that spark reflection and fresh ideas. When addressed wisely, disagreements can point out issues that need to improve. They can uncover unfairness, highlight new possibilities, or push people to understand each other better. In this chapter, we will look at how conflict can create positive change, the conditions needed for such change, and the methods that help groups and individuals learn and grow from disagreements.

By understanding how conflict can be a tool for improvement, you can shift from fearing it to seeing it as a chance to fix problems and build better relationships. This does not mean conflict is always pleasant. It does mean we can learn to use the energy inside a dispute for something constructive rather than destructive.

---

## 1. Recognizing the Value in Tension

It may seem strange to say conflict has value. Many of us were taught to think of conflict as purely bad or dangerous. Yet, tension often signals that something is out of balance and needs attention. Without this tension, people might ignore issues for a long time, letting problems remain.

- **Prompt to Examine Habits**: When a conflict erupts, it might show that a rule or routine no longer works. For example, family arguments about chores might reveal that the task plan is not fair.
- **Inspiration for New Ideas**: Different viewpoints can clash but also spark creativity. When coworkers debate how to handle a project, they might produce an unexpected, better plan.
- **Check on Respect**: Conflicts sometimes arise because someone feels disrespected or overlooked. This tension highlights the need to treat everyone fairly, so it can push a group to be more inclusive.
- **Chance to Communicate**: When conflict happens, people are motivated to talk about underlying issues. If handled with respect, these discussions can mend old wounds and prevent future disagreements.

Acknowledging that conflict can serve a purpose changes how we react. Instead of immediately trying to squash disagreements, we can see them as indicators of areas where growth may be needed.

## 2. Conflicts That Spark Positive Growth

Not all conflicts bring positive results. Some remain stuck in anger or lead to hurtful outcomes. However, certain patterns in conflict are more likely to inspire beneficial change:

1. **Both Sides Show Willingness to Listen**: If people choose to understand each other instead of winning at all costs, the conflict can transform into a shared problem-solving effort.
2. **Open Sharing of Information**: When facts, feelings, and perspectives are clearly exchanged, solutions are more realistic. Hidden agendas or secrets usually fuel more suspicion.
3. **Respectful Language**: Harsh insults block improvement, while calm words keep the door open for new ideas.
4. **Desire for Fairness**: Conflicts that focus on fairness or moral issues can lead to positive social changes. For instance, workers demanding fair pay might improve conditions for everyone if the employer agrees to discuss the issue sincerely.
5. **Safe Environment**: Where people feel physically and emotionally safe, they can share openly. In environments filled with fear or bullying, conflict is less likely to move in a good direction.

When these elements appear, a dispute has a good chance of leading to improvements rather than deeper divisions.

## 3. Examples of Positive Change from Conflict

### a) Family Reorganization

Imagine siblings always argue over the TV or shared devices. The conflict creates stress each evening. Eventually, parents and children come together and see that the root problem is a schedule that leaves one TV for many users. By brainstorming calmly, they decide to set a shared timetable, giving each person a fair slot. This conflict ends up reducing daily stress and helps them all learn to manage resources together.

**b) School Policy Improvements**

In a school, students might protest that the rules about lunch breaks are too restrictive. Teachers and administrators initially resist the students' complaints, seeing them as rebellious. But after a series of calm meetings—fueled by the ongoing conflict—the school agrees to adjust break times slightly. Students gain more time to eat and relax, which improves their focus in afternoon classes. The conflict led to a policy shift that benefits everyone.

**c) Workplace Innovation**

A company's engineering and marketing teams often clash about how to launch products. Marketing wants flashy ads, and engineering wants to make sure the product is fully tested. Their arguments get heated, but a manager suggests structured meetings where each side outlines goals and concerns clearly. The tension drives them to find a middle path: they decide on a limited but exciting early release that also includes robust testing. This approach boosts sales and quality, an outcome sparked by repeated conflict that demanded a fresh compromise.

**d) Community Accountability**

Neighbors may argue about noise or shared neighborhood spaces. If handled wisely—perhaps through community forums or a local mediator—these disputes can reveal that the neighborhood lacks clear guidelines on quiet hours or communal space usage. By creating new guidelines, the community reduces arguments and fosters a friendlier environment. This beneficial result would not have emerged without the initial conflict exposing the need.

In all these cases, disagreements became a signal that changes were necessary. The tension pushed people to fix underlying problems rather than ignoring them.

## 4. Shifting Our Mindset about Conflict

To harness positive change from conflict, we need to adjust how we see disagreements. Often, we treat conflict as a personal attack or a sign of failure. Shifting to a more constructive mindset involves:

- **Welcoming Honest Feedback**: Instead of dreading complaints or challenges, see them as information that helps you grow.
- **Admitting Imperfection**: No system or relationship is perfect. Conflict can highlight weaknesses, giving us chances to improve.
- **Reducing Fear of Discomfort**: Conflict can feel uncomfortable. But that discomfort can be the fuel that leads to breakthroughs.
- **Seeing Others as Partners**: Even if you disagree, viewing the other side as potential partners in problem-solving fosters cooperation.
- **Staying Curious**: Ask questions like, "What is making them so upset? Is there a fair solution we have not considered?" This curiosity can defuse anger and open the door to positive results.

By seeing conflict as an indicator rather than a catastrophe, we allow ourselves to use its energy for finding beneficial outcomes.

---

## 5. Personal Growth Through Conflict

Beyond the external changes conflict can create—like new rules or policies—there is also the internal change within ourselves. Disagreements test our patience, listening skills, self-control, and empathy. If we rise to the challenge:

1. **Stronger Emotional Control**: We learn to handle anger or frustration without lashing out, building resilience that helps in many parts of life.
2. **Better Communication Skills**: Repeated conflict resolution trains us to express ourselves clearly and listen more effectively.
3. **Higher Confidence**: Confronting disputes and solving them builds self-esteem, because we see we can handle tough situations.
4. **Deeper Self-Knowledge**: Conflict often exposes what truly matters to us. Through it, we learn our boundaries, triggers, and priorities more clearly.
5. **Broadening Perspectives**: Engaging respectfully with opposing views can expand our thinking, making us more flexible and wise.

These personal gains do not happen automatically; they require a willingness to reflect on each conflict and ask, "What did I learn?" But the rewards are significant, helping us become more capable individuals.

---

## 6. Group Transformation: Conflict as a Catalyst

In groups—like families, workplaces, or clubs—conflict can serve as a catalyst for group transformation. When done carefully, it can lead to:

- **Stronger Team Bonds**: Solving a major conflict together can build unity, similar to how teams can bond after overcoming a challenge.
- **Refined Goals or Missions**: Disagreement might show that the group's mission is unclear or outdated. By clarifying or updating it, the group becomes more focused.
- **New Leadership Approaches**: If a leader's style repeatedly causes friction, the conflict can force a shift to more balanced leadership methods.
- **Fairer Structures**: Groups might revise decision-making procedures, dividing tasks or power more evenly so that everyone feels included.
- **Enhanced Communication Norms**: A big conflict might prompt the group to agree on rules about how they communicate—like no interrupting, or giving each member a turn.

When groups adopt changes arising from conflict, they often experience renewed energy and clearer direction.

---

## 7. Steps to Turning Conflict into Positive Results

It is one thing to see the potential for conflict to create good outcomes and another to make it happen. Here is a path you can follow when a disagreement surfaces:

1. **Calm the Immediate Tension**: Use calm-down methods (breathing, short breaks, respectful tone) to prevent the conflict from becoming too heated.
2. **Identify the Core Issue**: Look beyond the surface argument. Ask, "What is really bothering each side? What problem keeps causing friction?"

3. **Speak Openly About Needs**: Each person (or group) clarifies what they need, not just what they do not want. This focuses on solutions.
4. **Brainstorm Multiple Solutions**: Gather ideas without judging them. Sometimes the best answer is a mix of different suggestions.
5. **Test and Adjust**: Agree to try a certain plan or change. Then monitor how it goes. If it does not fix the issue, return to the discussion to modify it.
6. **Reflect on Lessons**: Once the conflict cools, think about what you learned—both about the topic and your conflict resolution skills. This reflection cements the positive growth.

Following these steps can turn a heated argument into a process that identifies and addresses deeper concerns.

## 8. Avoiding Pitfalls that Block Positive Change

Not every conflict leads to improvement. Some remain stuck or even get worse. Several pitfalls can block beneficial outcomes:

- **Personal Attacks**: If the discussion focuses on personal failings rather than the issue, people become defensive, halting cooperation.
- **Blaming One Person Only**: Conflicts are often influenced by multiple factors. Pointing to one individual as the entire problem ignores deeper causes.
- **Refusing to Listen**: Growth happens when both sides share and hear each other. If one side shuts down discussion, the conflict stalls.
- **Winning at All Costs**: If someone only aims to "beat" the other side, no healthy solution emerges. Pride takes priority over fairness.
- **Immediate Overreaction**: Quick, drastic actions taken in anger or panic can cause damage, making things harder to repair later.

Being aware of these pitfalls helps you steer your conflicts toward a more positive direction. It is crucial to keep the bigger picture in mind: you want an outcome that improves conditions or relationships, not just a personal "win."

## 9. The Role of Empathy in Finding Good Outcomes

Empathy—trying to see and feel from another's perspective—fuels conflict transformation into something beneficial. When you apply empathy:

1. **You Spot Underlying Needs**: Perhaps a coworker is late to tasks because they are juggling a sick relative at home. Knowing this might lead to changes that help them cope, rather than simply labeling them as lazy.
2. **You Reduce Hostility**: Showing understanding often soothes the other person's anger, making them more open to your ideas.
3. **You Build Trust**: Empathy signals that you care about their well-being, not just about winning. This trust encourages them to share deeper concerns or vulnerabilities, which can be key to better solutions.
4. **You Expand Solution Options**: Once you grasp what truly matters to them, you can propose ideas that address both sides' real needs, not just the surface demands.

When conflict includes empathy, the path to a positive outcome becomes smoother and the final agreement is more likely to stick.

---

## 10. Learning from Conflict Failures to Improve Later

Sometimes, conflict does not end in a positive result. Maybe you gave in to anger, or the other side refused to talk. Or perhaps a forced agreement crumbled soon after. Even these "failures" can teach valuable lessons:

- **Identify Missed Chances**: Could you have invited a mediator earlier? Did you ignore a sign that the other person felt excluded?
- **See Personal Weak Spots**: Did you let pride block a compromise? Did you fail to manage your stress, leading to harsh words? Recognizing these patterns can help you plan better next time.
- **Seek Guidance**: If repeated conflicts end poorly, maybe outside help—a counselor or conflict coach—could guide you to handle future disputes more effectively.
- **Apologize and Repair**: Even if a conflict ended badly, you can still approach the other person later to say, "I regret how I acted. I want to see if we can find a better path." This might reopen the door to positive change.

Failure in one conflict does not doom you to repeat the same mistakes forever. By reflecting on what went wrong, you gain insights for handling future arguments more skillfully.

---

## 11. Conflict and Wider Social Change

Looking at history, big social changes often sprang from conflicts. Protests against unfair laws or fights for equal rights forced societies to question their rules. While large-scale conflicts can be stressful or even risky, many have led to important steps forward:

- **Worker Rights**: Labor movements worldwide used strikes (a form of conflict) to push for safer conditions and fair wages.
- **Civil Rights**: Disagreements about discrimination led to new laws protecting people from unfair treatment.
- **Environmental Protections**: Clashes between industries and conservation groups spurred regulations to keep air and water clean.

These examples show that conflict can go beyond personal relationships. When enough people see an issue and push for change, conflicts can reshape entire communities or nations for the better—again, provided the conflicts are guided by goals of fairness and respect, not merely chaos or violence.

---

## 12. Encouraging a Conflict-Positive Culture in Groups

If you are part of an organization—like a workplace, club, or community group—you can encourage a culture that sees conflict as a source of positive change:

1. **Train Members in Conflict Skills**: Offer short sessions on respectful discussion, active listening, and compromise.
2. **Establish Clear Processes**: Make sure everyone knows how to raise concerns and who to speak to about disputes.
3. **Praise Constructive Debate**: Acknowledge times when members disagree politely and find creative outcomes, showing that respectful disagreements are valued.

4. **Model Calm Leadership**: Leaders who remain calm and open to criticism set the tone. If a leader punishes dissent, the group will hide problems.
5. **Review Conflict Outcomes**: After a dispute is settled, briefly review how it was handled and what improvements resulted. This helps everyone learn.

Such measures create a supportive atmosphere where people do not fear being honest about problems. Then, instead of swirling silently, issues come forward sooner, letting the group address them before they explode.

---

## 13. Balancing Conflict and Harmony

While conflict can inspire progress, constant conflict is exhausting. Groups also need harmony and periods of agreement to function smoothly. Striking a balance:

- **Encourage Open Dialogue but Limit Personal Clashes**: Let members voice disagreements about ideas or policies, but discourage attacks on personal traits.
- **Focus on Shared Goals**: Remind everyone of common objectives. This turns conflicts into a quest for the best route to the same end, not a personal battle.
- **Alternate Between Exploration and Agreement**: Some meetings might focus on gathering conflicting views. Others might be about confirming decisions with less debate, giving the group a sense of forward momentum.
- **Use Conflict as a Periodic Check**: If conflict rarely appears, it might mean people are afraid to speak up. Periodic honest disagreements keep the group on its toes and adaptive.

In short, conflict should not be avoided entirely nor embraced blindly. Used thoughtfully, it becomes a tool for growth in a generally respectful environment.

---

## 14. Conflict and the Future: Building Lasting Solutions

When a conflict ends in a positive change, that is good. But to make sure the change remains helpful over time, consider these steps:

1. **Document Agreements**: Write down what each side agreed to do. This prevents memory-based disputes.
2. **Set Review Dates**: Plan a check-in after some weeks or months to see if the new arrangement or rule still works or needs adjusting.
3. **Stay Flexible**: If new issues pop up, do not be afraid to revise the agreement. A solution that worked in one phase might need tweaks later.
4. **Train New Members**: In workplaces or groups, new people might join who did not experience the conflict resolution. Brief them on the agreed norms so that the positive change continues.
5. **Keep Communication Channels Open**: After resolving one conflict, continue encouraging feedback so that small problems do not fester into big ones.

These steps ensure that conflict-driven improvements do not fade. Instead, they become part of a living, growing structure that benefits everyone.

---

## 15. Personal Stories: How Conflict Led to Growth

Below are short illustrations of individuals who grew because of conflict. These are hypothetical but reflect common real-life themes:

- **Rina**: She used to avoid any disagreement at work. When a major conflict arose over scheduling, she finally spoke up. Through that, she learned negotiation skills and realized her voice mattered. The schedule changed, and Rina felt more confident in all areas of her life.
- **Derrick**: A heated argument with a friend about financial responsibilities nearly ended their friendship. They decided to see a counselor together. That conflict forced Derrick to face his habit of avoiding bills. He changed his budgeting and repaid his friend, saving the friendship and improving his own financial habits.
- **Ashlee**: She had ongoing disputes with her teenage child about house rules. They rarely talked calmly. After repeated fights, Ashlee read about conflict resolution in families. She started holding weekly check-ins, giving each side a chance to speak. The arguments lessened, and her relationship with her child improved greatly.
- **Marcus**: As a group leader in a community project, he clashed with volunteers who disliked his style of decision-making. This conflict led

Marcus to learn facilitation skills, letting everyone contribute. The project flourished because volunteers felt heard and committed.

In all these examples, conflict was uncomfortable—but it awakened a need to learn, adapt, or address a blind spot. That process led to stronger skills, improved relationships, or better habits.

---

## 16. Teaching Youth the Concept of Conflict as Opportunity

Parents, educators, or mentors can teach children and teens to see conflict as something they can learn from, rather than something to fear or fight blindly:

- **Use Simple Words**: Explain that arguments show we have different ideas or needs, and that finding fair solutions can help everyone.
- **Role-Play**: Practice scenarios where kids disagree, then show how to handle it calmly. Ask them how they might improve a rule or routine.
- **Highlight Success Stories**: Share real or fictional stories where children overcame disagreements and made things better.
- **Encourage Problem-Solving**: If siblings argue, guide them to suggest solutions. Over time, they see conflict as solvable, not terrifying.
- **Praise Growth**: When a child resolves a conflict in a positive way, point out what they did well: "You stayed calm and listened to your sister's idea."

Growing up with this mindset helps them carry a healthier attitude toward disagreements into adulthood.

---

## 17. Handling Conflict While Maintaining Positivity

A big challenge in conflict is balancing realism (knowing disagreements can be tough) with optimism (believing they can lead to good changes). Some tips:

- **Acknowledge the Difficulty**: It is okay to admit a conflict is draining or emotional. That does not mean it cannot turn out well.
- **Focus on Solutions, Not Failures**: Avoid dwelling too long on who made past mistakes. Shift to "What can we do now to fix this?"

- **Point Out Progress**: If the conflict used to make everyone shout, but now people are at least talking calmly, that is a positive step. Keep building on such progress.
- **Keep a Light Tone if Appropriate**: Gentle humor or a friendly approach can stop the conflict from feeling hopeless, as long as you do not trivialize real concerns.
- **Seek Support**: If negativity takes over, get help from someone who can remind you of possible ways forward.

Staying positive in the face of tension does not mean ignoring real problems. It means believing that conflicts can be transformed into steps forward with careful handling.

---

## 18. The Importance of Follow-Through

Many people reach an agreement during or after conflict but fail to keep it going. Without follow-through, potential positive change fades:

- **Set Specific Tasks**: If you agree to do something (like take out the trash on certain days or meet a work deadline earlier), be clear on the details.
- **Mark Checkpoints**: In a family or team, maybe review the agreement each week to confirm it is happening. This consistent review builds trust.
- **Be Accountable**: If you slip up, admit it quickly and try to correct it. That honesty can preserve the spirit of the new arrangement.
- **Encourage Each Other**: In a group, noticing small successes in keeping the agreement can motivate everyone to stay committed.
- **Refine As Needed**: If a plan turns out to have flaws, return to the discussion calmly. Adjusting an agreement is better than abandoning it.

Follow-through is the difference between a conflict resolution that only looks good on paper and one that truly changes behaviors or conditions.

# Chapter 19: Keeping Peace in Groups

Groups are part of our daily lives—families, friend circles, classrooms, sports teams, clubs, workplaces, and neighborhood committees. Each group includes people with unique personalities, goals, and styles of communication. Because of this variety, disagreements often arise. One person might think a certain activity is fun, while another finds it a waste of time. A few people might want to make decisions quickly, while others prefer careful deliberation. Someone might handle stress quietly, while another might share every worry out loud. All these differences can spark conflict.

However, groups also offer big advantages. They let us combine strengths, share ideas, and support each other. When a group maintains peace, it can function smoothly, build strong relationships, and reach shared objectives more successfully. Keeping peace does not mean never disagreeing. Instead, it means learning to handle disagreements in a respectful, orderly way so that nobody feels scared or left out. This chapter will look at why group conflicts happen, how to prevent them, and ways to handle disputes before they grow too big. By the end, you will have tools to help your group remain cohesive even when members do not always see eye to eye.

---

## 1. Why Group Conflicts Arise

Groups naturally mix different viewpoints, experiences, and priorities. These differences can be an asset but also lead to disagreements. Some common reasons include:

1. **Varied Personalities**: People who are very talkative might dominate discussions, while quiet members feel unseen. Or a strong-willed personality might clash with someone more flexible.
2. **Different Goals**: Even if the overall purpose is shared (like winning a sports event), each person might have a personal goal. For instance, one wants to practice a lot, another wants just to have fun.
3. **Communication Gaps**: In bigger groups, messages can get lost. One group might decide on a plan but forget to tell everyone. Such gaps breed confusion and conflict.

4. **Resource Competition**: Whether it is budget, time on a shared computer, or even space in a meeting room, limited resources often create tensions.
5. **Uneven Effort**: In teams, some might work very hard, while others slack off. This imbalance leads to resentment and arguments over fairness.
6. **Leadership Disputes**: Who gets to be in charge? People might compete for leadership, or a leader might make choices that others dislike.

These triggers appear in everything from after-school clubs to large companies. When a group is aware of them, it can watch for early signs of friction. Catching small issues soon is easier than letting them grow into major conflicts.

---

## 2. Setting a Foundation for Peace

The best strategy for keeping peace is creating an environment that prevents many conflicts from starting. If a group has strong communication, fair guidelines, and mutual respect, disagreements are less likely to turn ugly. Key steps include:

**a) Clear Purpose and Goals**
A group that knows its main aims is less prone to random disputes. For example, a volunteer committee might say, "Our goal is to organize a local clean-up day to help the environment." With that purpose in mind, all members can evaluate ideas by asking, "Does this serve our goal?" If suggestions stray too far, they can redirect gently without personal attacks.

**b) Agreed Communication Rules**
Groups that function well usually have ground rules for talking to each other. These might include:

- No interrupting when someone has the floor.
- Everyone gets a chance to share.
- Keep words respectful, avoiding insults or personal digs.
- If a topic gets heated, the group can pause for a breath or a quick break.

When everyone knows these rules and sees them enforced, members feel safer expressing concerns. It also reduces the chance of a single loud voice dominating.

### c) Defined Roles and Responsibilities

Clarity about who does what prevents overlap or confusion. For instance, in a school project group, decide who researches, who writes, who creates visuals, and who presents. Everyone sees their tasks and respects that others have different tasks. This clarity reduces arguments over whether someone is "stepping on my territory" or "not doing enough."

### d) Inclusive Decision-Making

If decisions always come from one or two people, others might feel ignored. A more inclusive approach—like voting, rotating leadership, or discussion-based agreement—helps each member feel invested. This investment lowers resentment and encourages cooperation, because people know they have a say.

### e) Trust-Building Activities

Groups often bond better if they share small moments of fun or casual interaction. This can be as simple as starting each meeting with a quick, light-hearted check-in or game. These positive experiences build trust, making it easier for members to talk problems through calmly rather than jump to blame.

With these measures in place, many conflicts can be prevented. Still, some disagreements will happen naturally, so the group also needs methods to handle them when they appear.

---

## 3. Recognizing Early Signs of Tension

Groups rarely explode in conflict out of nowhere. Usually, small warning signs appear first:

1. **Body Language Shifts**: People might roll their eyes, cross their arms, or lean away when certain topics arise.
2. **Side Conversations**: If members start whispering or texting each other about group issues instead of speaking openly, frustration may be building.
3. **Drop in Attendance**: If a group meets regularly and some members start skipping, they might feel disengaged or upset.
4. **Complaints Outside Meetings**: A member might grumble to a friend about unfairness but never mention it to the group.

5. **Sudden Silence**: Someone who used to contribute might withdraw, possibly because they feel overshadowed or upset.

When group leaders or attentive members notice these clues, they can address them early. For instance, they might ask, "Would you like to share any concerns you have about the plan? We want to hear all viewpoints." That direct, gentle invitation often helps a frustrated person speak up before emotions boil over.

---

## 4. Handling Minor Disagreements Quickly

Minor disagreements are easier to fix if tackled soon. For example, if two group members have different opinions on a small matter (like the color scheme for a project poster), they can:

- **Discuss Right Away**: Let them chat briefly after the meeting to find a quick compromise.
- **Keep It Friendly**: Remind them that this is a small part of the overall goal. Sometimes a short talk about pros and cons is enough.
- **Listen to Each Other**: Even if the matter seems trivial, a member might care deeply for personal reasons. Hearing them out can prevent bigger resentments.
- **Check Group Preferences If Needed**: If they cannot decide, ask others to weigh in or hold a quick vote. This stops the matter from lingering.

Nipping small clashes in the bud keeps them from morphing into bigger resentments. It also sets an example that it is normal to handle little disputes openly and courteously.

---

## 5. Group Conflict Resolution Steps

Sometimes, a disagreement involves more than one or two people, or it touches on core issues like leadership or money. In these cases, the group might use a structured conflict resolution process:

1. **Agree to a Calm Discussion**: The group decides on a time and place to talk, with an understanding that this is a safe, respectful space.

2. **Define the Problem**: Each side shares their view of the issue. The aim is to clarify what is causing the conflict. Maybe the group's budget is too tight for all proposed projects, leading to disputes about priorities.
3. **Gather Information**: Check facts and figures. If the conflict is about scheduling, look at everyone's availability. If it is about money, bring accurate budget data.
4. **Let All Voices Be Heard**: Use a fair process, like giving each person a set time. The rest listen without interrupting.
5. **Look for Underlying Needs**: Is the real problem that one subgroup feels their ideas are never taken seriously? Or that someone's role is unclear? Pinpointing the deeper concern helps a more lasting solution.
6. **Brainstorm Solutions**: Invite all members to propose ideas. Write them down without judging right away.
7. **Evaluate and Choose**: Discuss which ideas meet the group's goals and each side's needs. If possible, pick or combine solutions that the majority can support.
8. **Confirm and Assign Tasks**: If the solution involves changing a schedule or plan, decide who updates it, who communicates it, etc. Make the changes official.
9. **Follow Up**: After a set time, review if the agreement is working. Tweak it if needed.

This structured approach keeps the discussion from descending into random arguments. By focusing on the issue and possible fixes, the group harnesses conflict energy into real progress.

---

## 6. The Role of Leadership in Maintaining Peace

Leaders, whether formal (like a manager or club president) or informal (a respected member), play a huge part in group harmony. A leader who dismisses concerns or punishes disagreement can worsen tensions. On the other hand, a positive leader:

- **Models Respect**: They speak calmly, listen to others, and refrain from shaming or humiliating members.
- **Facilitates Fair Processes**: They ensure no one is silenced, that tasks are balanced, and that any conflict is addressed promptly.

- **Promotes Transparency**: Sharing information about decisions or finances can reduce suspicion.
- **Supports Skill Development**: Encouraging members to learn communication and problem-solving skills fosters independence.
- **Accepts Feedback**: Leaders who welcome feedback (even if it is critical) set the tone that disagreements are safe to discuss.

When a leader fosters these habits, group members often follow suit. Conversely, if a leader is controlling, rude, or secretive, group conflict is more likely to grow.

---

## 7. Dealing with Dominant or Aggressive Members

Some group members may have strong personalities or come across as aggressive. They might talk loudly, interrupt others, or insist on their ideas without listening. While these individuals can bring energy or expertise, they also risk stifling others. To keep the group peaceful:

- **Enforce Discussion Rules**: The group can have a rule: "Everyone has two minutes to speak before we move on." If a dominant member interrupts, the facilitator reminds them politely.
- **Encourage Turn-Taking**: The facilitator or leader might say, "We have not heard from Sam yet. Let's let Sam speak now."
- **Speak Privately if Needed**: If the person frequently disrupts, a leader or a respected member can talk to them one-on-one: "Your ideas matter, but we also need to hear from everyone else. Can we find a way to ensure all voices are included?"
- **Highlight Positives**: A strong-willed member may have valuable contributions, so it helps to acknowledge that. Then guide them to collaborate rather than dominate.
- **Consider Mediation**: If this behavior persists, a neutral mediator can step in to help the entire group develop better communication norms.

Addressing aggressive behavior early prevents resentment from building among quieter or overshadowed members. It also shows the group values balanced participation.

## 8. Conflict in Large Groups or Committees

Larger groups have more complexity: more voices, more subgroups, and more potential for confusion. To keep the peace in a large setting:

1. **Use Smaller Breakouts**: Divide into sub-teams focusing on specific tasks or topics. Each sub-team solves its minor disputes, then reports back. This makes it easier to handle details without overwhelming the entire group.
2. **Appoint Facilitators or Moderators**: These individuals guide discussions, track time, and ensure fairness. In very large meetings, multiple facilitators might handle different sections.
3. **Create Clear Documentation**: Meeting agendas, minutes, and action items help everyone see the same information. This documentation reduces misunderstandings about decisions.
4. **Rotate Responsibilities**: Let different members host or lead certain parts of meetings. This spreads leadership and prevents power struggles.
5. **Set Time for Feedback**: Large groups can hold short Q&A or feedback sessions at the end of each meeting. This provides space for concerns before they grow.

These approaches help keep large groups focused and organized, minimizing chaos that leads to conflict. If a major dispute surfaces, the group can form a smaller conflict-resolution team to address it carefully.

---

## 9. Cultural Differences in Group Conflict

In diverse groups, cultural norms may clash. For instance, some cultures find it polite to speak softly and avoid direct confrontation, while others view directness as honest. Some place big importance on seniority or hierarchy, while others prefer equal participation for all members. Such differences can produce confusion or tension:

- **Encourage Cultural Awareness**: Groups can set aside time to discuss and understand each other's backgrounds.
- **Use Neutral Conflict Processes**: Structured methods that everyone agrees on can reduce confusion over "the right way" to disagree. For

example, a "talking piece" in a circle, where only the person holding the item speaks, can feel fair to members from various cultures.
- **Watch for Misinterpretations**: A loud voice might be normal in someone's culture, while others see it as aggression. Or avoiding eye contact might be a sign of respect in one tradition, but suspicion in another. By checking assumptions, the group avoids labeling each other unfairly.
- **Seek Professional Mediation if Needed**: In deeply diverse groups or if strong cultural conflicts arise, a mediator who understands cross-cultural communication can help.

Respecting cultural differences is vital for peace. When a group embraces these differences, it gains richer perspectives, although it must work harder to align communication styles.

---

## 10. Conflict Over Roles and Leadership

Sometimes, group peace is threatened by disputes about who leads or how leaders are chosen. This can occur when:

- **Leadership Is Unclear**: If no one is sure who is in charge, chaos and power grabs may ensue.
- **Leader Holds Too Much Power**: A leader might ignore input, leading to frustrated group members.
- **Multiple Leaders**: Two or more people may be recognized as leaders, creating competing directions.

To address leadership conflicts:

- **Decide on a Leadership Structure**: If it is a formal group, hold proper elections or appoint people for specific terms. If it is informal, talk openly about who will coordinate tasks.
- **Distribute Authority**: Instead of one person making all decisions, create a small committee for certain areas or rotate leadership duties.
- **Regular Check-Ins with the Leader**: The group can schedule times to give feedback to the leader and confirm they are representing everyone's interests.

- **Clarity on the Leader's Role**: Is the leader a facilitator, a final decision-maker, or something else? People must know to avoid unrealistic expectations.
- **Allow Leader Transitions**: If a leader steps down or is replaced, plan a smooth transition so that the new person can take over without confusion.

A group that manages leadership transitions fairly and clearly often remains stable, even if conflicts arise over direction or style.

---

## 11. Overcoming Groupthink and Fear of Disagreement

Sometimes the group's problem is not too much conflict, but too little. Members might fear speaking up if they sense the majority disagrees, creating "groupthink," where everyone pretends to agree just to maintain harmony. This can hide real concerns, which later explode into major conflict.

- **Encourage Dissenting Opinions**: Let people know it is safe to disagree. A phrase like, "If anyone sees a flaw in this plan, please speak up," invites alternative views.
- **Assign a "Devil's Advocate"**: In some meetings, one person's role is to question decisions on purpose. This normalizes disagreement.
- **Use Anonymous Feedback**: If members fear direct confrontation, allow a suggestion box, an anonymous poll, or a digital survey.
- **Acknowledge All Contributions**: Thank people who raise concerns. This shows the group values honesty over forced agreement.
- **Check for Pressure**: If a leader or a strong member is pushing everyone to say yes, talk privately about how forced consensus can harm real progress.

Healthy conflict can help the group find stronger solutions. Stopping people from voicing concerns might keep things calm on the surface, but it often leads to bigger issues later.

---

## 12. Handling Cliques and Subgroups

In larger groups, smaller friend circles or sub-teams can turn into cliques that exclude others. They might share inside jokes, protect each other's interests, or block outside ideas. This creates us-versus-them attitudes that disrupt group peace.

- **Mix Groupings**: Occasionally shuffle who works together on tasks, preventing fixed cliques from always forming.
- **Encourage Shared Activities**: If possible, have some gatherings where people mingle outside their usual cliques.
- **Promote Inclusive Language**: Leaders can remind members not to use coded or inside terms that leave newcomers confused.
- **Address Clique Behavior**: If a specific clique refuses to include others, gently talk with them or hold a group discussion about how everyone can feel welcome.
- **Recognize Achievements Across Subgroups**: If the group praises only one subgroup's efforts, others can feel sidelined. Ensuring balanced appreciation helps all sub-teams feel valued.

Cliques are not always bad; they can represent friendships. But left unchecked, they undermine unity. By mixing people up and emphasizing shared identity, the group keeps a friendly atmosphere for everyone.

---

## 13. Conflict in Virtual or Remote Groups

Many groups now operate partly or fully online. Remote collaboration introduces unique challenges for keeping peace:

- **Limited Nonverbal Cues**: Text chats or emails lack tone of voice or facial expressions, so misunderstandings can occur.
- **Different Time Zones**: A group spread around the world might have trouble scheduling real-time talks. This can delay conflict resolution.
- **Tech Glitches**: Connection problems can frustrate members, creating tension that spills into conflict.
- **Lack of Casual Bonds**: Without casual in-person chats or breaks, members can feel less personal connection, leading to quicker anger.

To address these:

1. **Video or Voice Calls**: Use these rather than only text for sensitive topics. Hearing voices and seeing faces can reduce misinterpretation.
2. **Scheduled Communication**: Decide on certain times when everyone is available for quick discussions. This avoids drawn-out text debates.
3. **Clarity in Writing**: When using email or chat, keep messages concise and polite. If something could be misunderstood, clarify it or add a gentle note to show your tone.
4. **Digital Team-Building**: Plan short virtual "coffee breaks" or fun chats where people can connect informally, building trust.
5. **Be Patient with Tech Issues**: If someone's connection drops, do not get angry. Show understanding that remote setups can have hiccups.

While remote work can make conflict trickier, mindful communication and empathy still go a long way to keep groups peaceful.

---

## 14. Strategies for Long-Term Group Harmony

If your group meets over months or years, it is vital to maintain stability:

### a) Regular Check-Ins
Hold short sessions where each member says what is going well and what concerns them. This consistent practice can reveal tensions early. People might mention, "I feel overshadowed during design discussions" or "We are missing deadlines because tasks are unclear." Handling these concerns as they come up stops them from becoming major conflicts.

### b) Celebrating Wins
When the group accomplishes something, acknowledging or marking that success fosters positive feelings and unity. For instance, after finishing a fundraiser, the group might share a quick reflection on what worked well. However, do not let this overshadow remaining issues. Balance positivity with honesty about areas to improve.

### c) Training in Conflict Skills
Even if the group has no big conflict now, scheduling a workshop on communication or conflict resolution can be beneficial. This builds readiness for when a challenge does occur.

### d) Transparent Records

Keep logs of decisions, budgets, roles, and deadlines in a shared space. This reduces confusion and suspicion. If a member wants to see how a decision was made or how funds are spent, they can do so without secretiveness.

### e) Flexible Structure

As people come and go, or as goals change, the group's structure might need to adjust. A rigid system that worked before might cause conflict when the group grows or shifts focus. Being open to reviewing and revising the structure periodically prevents stale processes from sparking resentment.

---

## 15. Dealing with Repeated Offenders

Sometimes, a group member repeatedly causes trouble—missing deadlines, insulting others, or ignoring agreed rules. If the group tries to fix it but sees no change, the tension remains high. Steps to consider:

1. **Private Conversations**: A leader or a mediator can talk to them individually: "We have noticed a pattern in how you interact with others. We want to hear your side and see if we can address it."
2. **Set Consequences**: If the group has agreed rules, it also needs consequences for violating them. For instance, repeated offensive remarks might lead to suspension from the group for a certain period.
3. **Offer Support**: Perhaps the person struggles with personal issues or lacks certain skills. The group could offer to help them find resources or training to improve behavior.
4. **Involve the Whole Group**: If private efforts fail, a group meeting might be called. Be sure to keep it respectful, focusing on specific behaviors rather than attacking the person.
5. **Final Measures**: In extreme cases, removing the person from the group might be necessary for overall peace, though that is generally a last resort.

While these steps can be awkward, ignoring a repeatedly disruptive member can harm morale and drive away dedicated participants.

## 16. Balancing Individual Desires and Group Needs

A group must meet collective aims but also respect each member's rights and interests. Conflict often arises when one side emphasizes personal wishes, while the other side worries about what the group as a whole needs. Finding balance:

- **Respect Individual Opinions**: Everyone has the right to express how they feel or what they want, even if the group cannot fulfill every preference.
- **Explain Group Constraints**: If the group cannot accommodate all requests (lack of funds, limited time), clearly state these limitations so members understand the reasoning.
- **Seek Win-Win Options**: For instance, if a team member wants more creative freedom, but the group must maintain brand consistency, maybe they can design a special side project that still fits brand guidelines.
- **Rotate Responsibilities**: People who often follow others' decisions might want a turn leading an activity. This rotation can keep them engaged and valued.
- **Keep Communication Channels Open**: Check with members individually sometimes: "Do you feel your needs are being heard? Is there anything we can adjust?"

Balancing individual and group priorities can be tricky, but it reduces feelings of neglect or oppression, thus preserving harmony.

---

## 17. Building Emotional Safety in Group Settings

Emotional safety means members feel they can be themselves without fear of mocking, backlash, or punishment. When a group fosters emotional safety:

1. **Members Share Ideas Freely**: Even if an idea is unusual, people do not fear ridicule. That open climate promotes creativity.
2. **Conflicts Are Handled Gently**: People dare to voice disagreements since they trust the group will address them kindly, not retaliate.
3. **Apologies Happen**: If someone says or does something hurtful, they can admit it, and the group forgives, moving forward together.
4. **Feedback is Given Constructively**: Critiques come with care, focusing on actions or tasks, not personal traits.

5. **Less Defensive Behavior**: Because members feel safe, they are less likely to become defensive or lash out.

Leaders and senior members can model this by handling their own mistakes openly, welcoming questions, and praising genuine communication efforts. Over time, emotional safety becomes a shared norm.

---

## 18. The Power of Group Reflection After Conflict

Once a group conflict is resolved, reflection can make the solution last and help members improve. This is similar to how an individual might reflect, but on a group level:

- **Organize a Debrief Meeting**: The group sets aside time specifically to discuss what happened, how they solved it, and what they learned.
- **Encourage Honest Thoughts**: Each member can share how they felt during the conflict. This can clear lingering misunderstandings.
- **Highlight the Positive Outcome**: If the group discovered a better process or new rule, note how it helps the group.
- **Note What Could Improve**: Perhaps the group took too long to address the issue, or communication channels were not well managed. Outline steps to fix those parts.
- **Keep a Record**: Summarize the main points in writing so future members or leaders can learn from it.

This reflection fosters continuous growth. The group becomes more confident in handling future disputes, aware of what works and what to avoid.

---

# Chapter 20: Looking Ahead to Ongoing Harmony

As you reach the end of this book, you have explored many sides of conflict—why it happens, how emotions drive it, how communication and empathy can address it, and how it can lead to positive changes. You have learned to calm yourself, speak respectfully, seek help when needed, and handle group challenges. Yet the real test of conflict resolution skills comes over time, as life presents new disputes, new contexts, and new relationships. This final chapter focuses on how to carry these lessons forward in a lasting way.

Lasting harmony is not about never having conflict. It is about creating conditions where problems are tackled early, solutions are sought fairly, and people stay open to continuous growth. Whether at home, in school, at work, or in the broader community, your ongoing efforts to handle conflict wisely will help you and those around you live with greater peace. This chapter will offer suggestions for keeping your conflict resolution skills strong, adapting to changing situations, and ensuring that the patterns of respect and empathy become permanent features of your life.

---

## 1. Conflict as a Normal Part of Life

One of the biggest shifts you can make is accepting conflict as normal. This does not mean welcoming endless drama, but recognizing that disagreements arise in all human communities. Viewing conflict as a chance to fix issues instead of a personal attack helps you stay calm and objective:

- **Maintain a Positive Outlook**: If you approach conflict expecting a destructive fight, you might unknowingly create that reality. If you expect a chance to learn or find solutions, you keep your mind open.
- **Stay Centered on the Topic**: Conflict is less frightening if you see it as "We have a problem to solve together" rather than "This person is my enemy."
- **Resist Shame**: It is common to feel shame or embarrassment when conflict appears, as though you or the group has failed. Remember that conflict is inevitable when people care deeply or hold varied viewpoints.
- **Use Conflicts to Grow**: Each argument or dispute can teach you more about emotional control, negotiation, and empathy—strengthening you for future situations.

Changing your default mindset about conflict does not happen overnight, but each time you handle a disagreement maturely, you reinforce the habit of seeing conflict as manageable, not terrifying.

## 2. Keeping Your Skills Sharp

You have gathered many tools: active listening, "I" statements, calming techniques, structured problem-solving, empathy, and more. But these skills can fade if you do not use them regularly. To keep them sharp:

1. **Apply Them Daily**: Even small frustrations at home, like who washes the dishes, can be an opportunity to practice calm communication and a focus on needs.
2. **Observe Others**: Watch how people around you (in real life or media) handle conflict. Identify what they do well or poorly. This observation reminds you of effective strategies.
3. **Teach Someone Else**: Sharing a skill like active listening with a friend or sibling helps cement it in your own mind.
4. **Refine Methods**: Maybe you learned a breathing technique that works half the time. Try variations or look up new tips to boost its effectiveness.
5. **Join or Start a Peer Group**: If you are in a setting where such a group can exist, gather people who also want to improve conflict resolution. You can swap experiences and suggestions.

Keeping conflict resolution in your thoughts, even in small ways, ensures it remains a natural part of how you address problems.

## 3. Planning for Changes and Surprises

Life brings changes—a new job, moving cities, new family members, shifting friendships. Each change can spark fresh conflicts, so planning helps:

- **Expect Tension During Transitions**: If you move in with new roommates, do not wait for a disagreement. Propose a meeting to discuss cleaning, bills, or overnight guests from the start.
- **Stay Alert for New Triggers**: A new work environment might have different rules or personalities. Identify potential conflict sources early—such as unclear deadlines or competing teams.

- **Set Boundaries**: When entering a new relationship or group, clarify your boundaries calmly. For instance, "I need a quiet hour in the evening to concentrate on my studies."
- **Keep Communication Channels Open**: If you sense confusion or tension building, address it soon. Quick talks often prevent bigger issues.
- **Seek Advice from People Who Know the Context**: If you are new to a community or job, ask someone who has been there about common conflicts or norms. That knowledge can guide you around pitfalls.

By preparing for changes instead of reacting in panic, you remain proactive. This mindset allows you to shape new environments in ways that reduce unnecessary disputes.

---

## 4. Balancing Forgiveness and Boundaries

Conflict resolution often involves forgiving mistakes—both your own and others'. However, forgiveness does not mean allowing harmful patterns to continue. It can be tricky to balance:

- **Healthy Forgiveness**: Recognize that people can grow. If someone apologized and changed their behavior, forgiving them can heal emotional wounds.
- **Setting Firm Boundaries**: If they keep hurting you or show no real regret, do not keep giving them infinite chances. You can forgive the past but maintain distance to protect yourself.
- **Learning from Each Conflict**: Even if you forgive, pay attention to warning signs. If a coworker repeatedly ignores your requests for personal space, forgiving them does not mean ignoring the problem again and again.
- **Self-Forgiveness**: We all slip up. If you handled a conflict poorly, reflect on the lesson, then let go of guilt. Dwelling on past mistakes can freeze you, preventing future improvement.

This balance ensures you remain open-hearted without becoming a target for continuous harm.

---

## 5. Sustaining Harmony in Families

Family dynamics can be especially emotional because members share living space or deep bonds. Maintaining long-term peace after learning these skills means:

1. **Family Meetings**: Continue holding short, regular meetings where everyone can bring up concerns. This forms a habit of open communication.
2. **Rotating Leadership**: If it is a household with older kids, sometimes let them set the meeting agenda or run a discussion. This teaches them responsibility and fairness.
3. **Respect Each Person's Growth**: Kids become teens, teens become adults, parents age, and roles shift. Acknowledge these changes so new conflicts do not arise from outdated assumptions.
4. **Shared Chores or Finances**: If a conflict was about chores or money, keep using fair systems. If the system stops working, discuss updates, not blame.
5. **Handling Big Life Events**: Marriage, divorce, moves, or illness can upset family routines. Bring out your conflict resolution toolkit proactively to handle the added stress and keep peace.

By consistently applying calm talk, empathy, and solutions, families build trust. Each member sees that the household can face disagreements while remaining supportive.

---

## 6. Sustaining Harmony in Friendships

Friend groups shift over time as people develop new interests, move away, or face life events. Avoid letting small conflicts or misunderstandings drive friends apart:

- **Check-Ins**: Occasionally ask friends how they feel about group outings or the balance of give-and-take in the friendship. Sometimes, a friend might be too polite to speak up about feeling left out unless asked.
- **Honoring Boundaries**: If a friend sets a boundary—like being unable to meet late at night—respect it. Forcing them or guilt-tripping can lead to hidden resentments.

- **Open to Apologies**: Mistakes happen. A friend might say something hurtful or break a promise. Forgive them if they show genuine regret, while also letting them know how you felt.
- **Nonviolent Communication**: This method uses empathy, observation (not judgments), and requests (not demands). For instance, "I notice you have been canceling plans. Are you feeling stressed? I really enjoy spending time with you and hope we can figure out a schedule that works."
- **Accepting Natural Changes**: Some friendships do fade if life paths diverge. You can handle that calmly rather than letting conflicts over your differences tear you apart.

When friends remain honest and caring, conflicts become chances to strengthen their bond rather than end it.

---

## 7. Sustaining Harmony in Workplaces

Your conflict resolution abilities are vital on the job, where many personalities and tasks intertwine:

1. **Regular Team Huddles**: Brief check-ins (sometimes daily or weekly) let people share updates or concerns. This open line can stop small workplace issues from growing.
2. **Clear Role Definitions**: Keep job descriptions updated and confirm them with team members. Reducing role confusion limits arguments about responsibility.
3. **Constructive Feedback Culture**: Encourage employees to give each other helpful suggestions rather than silent grudges or harsh criticism. In some workplaces, "feedback rounds" are scheduled to keep it organized.
4. **Encourage Skill Development**: Workshops on emotional intelligence, negotiation, or stress management help employees handle tension. Well-trained staff create a friendlier, more cooperative environment.
5. **Fair Dispute Procedures**: If conflicts arise and cannot be solved informally, having a known process—like contacting HR or a mediator—ensures everyone knows where to turn.

Workplaces that invest in conflict resolution see fewer resignations due to drama or burnout, leading to higher morale and productivity. Your personal example of calm and empathy can influence colleagues and managers.

## 8. Keeping Conflict Resolution Alive in Schools

Whether you are a student, parent, or teacher, the lessons in conflict resolution matter a lot in schools, which are busy environments with academic pressure and social dynamics:

- **Peer Mediation Programs**: Schools that train students to mediate peer conflicts see a reduction in fights and bullying. If you have the chance, support or join such programs.
- **Class Agreements**: Teachers and students can create shared classroom rules about respect, talking turns, and how to handle disagreements.
- **Teachers as Models**: A teacher who stays calm when a student acts out shows the class that anger can be managed. Students learn from that example daily.
- **Anti-Bullying Initiatives**: Clear anti-bullying policies, along with steps for reporting and addressing incidents, create a safer climate.
- **Promoting Empathy in Lessons**: Some schools integrate empathy and communication training into the curriculum, teaching kids from a young age that conflict can be resolved nonviolently.

A school committed to peaceful conflict resolution shapes future adults who handle disagreements responsibly, both at home and in society.

---

## 9. Community and Neighborhood Peace

Beyond families, workplaces, and schools, entire neighborhoods or towns can benefit from conflict resolution methods:

- **Community Meetings**: Local residents gather to discuss concerns (noise, safety, shared facilities). Using respectful procedures helps avoid heated shouting matches.
- **Neighborhood Mediation Centers**: Some cities have free or low-cost centers where trained mediators help neighbors settle disputes over property lines or noise, rather than taking it to court.
- **Volunteer Groups**: Residents might form volunteer committees to improve local areas. When conflicts arise, these committees can apply the same steps: calm talk, active listening, collaboration.

- **Cultural Exchanges**: In diverse communities, organizing open houses or cultural events fosters mutual understanding. Conflicts often fade when neighbors get to know each other personally.
- **Posting Clear Guidelines**: If a neighborhood park has rules for usage, posting them reduces confusion. Disagreements about dog walking or loud music can be solved more easily if rules are known.

These actions build a sense of unity and reduce tension. Your personal conflict resolution approach can spark new ideas or help your community handle tensions constructively.

---

## 10. Applying Skills to Broader Social Issues

Sometimes, conflict arises around social or political topics. While big issues like political elections or social justice can feel overwhelming, the same fundamental skills help:

1. **Active Listening to Opposing Views**: This fosters understanding, even if you strongly disagree. People rarely change their stance if they feel attacked. Listening respectfully might open channels to common ground.
2. **Staying Calm During Heated Debates**: Political conversations can get fiery. Using breathing techniques, calm speech, and respectful language sets you apart from polarizing shouting matches.
3. **Seeking Shared Values**: People might differ on how to solve a problem, yet share a belief in fairness or well-being for everyone. Identifying that shared value can lessen hostility.
4. **Focusing on Real Data**: In big debates, facts can be twisted. Searching reliable information, verifying sources, and calmly sharing them can reduce emotional misunderstandings.
5. **Knowing When to Pause**: If a debate is going nowhere, step back. Offer to revisit it later or to explore it with a mediator or a well-structured group forum.

You may not fix all global conflicts, but on a local scale, these approaches can keep your discussions about important topics from deteriorating into resentment and can encourage more thoughtful community dialogue.

## 11. Staying Motivated in the Face of Recurring Conflicts

Some conflicts reappear, especially in families or longtime friend groups. This can be discouraging if you feel you keep solving the same argument. To stay motivated:

- **Remember Progress**: Even if the issue returns, maybe it reappeared less intensely, or you resolved it faster this time. That is still progress.
- **Spot Patterns**: Is there a cyclical root cause? Maybe every holiday, relatives fight about the same topics. Identifying triggers helps you prepare or alter the environment.
- **Seek Deeper Solutions**: Repeated conflicts might point to an underlying issue never fully addressed—like old grudges, mental health challenges, or core value differences. Addressing the root is tougher but more lasting.
- **Consider Professional Guidance**: If you are stuck in a loop, therapy, counseling, or a specialized mediator might break the cycle.

Over time, repeated issues can slowly diminish if the group remains persistent about identifying deeper causes and improving communication.

---

## 12. Passing Conflict Skills to Others

One way to ensure these approaches last is to share them with new people—friends, relatives, or younger generations:

- **Explain Basics**: Teach them simple steps like using "I" statements, taking a break to calm down, and listening fully.
- **Demonstrate**: Let them see you handle a real disagreement calmly. If they witness you staying patient under stress, that lesson sticks.
- **Encourage Their Growth**: If a child or friend tries to solve conflict in a healthy manner, acknowledge that effort. Constructive feedback helps them keep learning.
- **Suggest Resources**: Recommend books, articles, or short workshops on conflict resolution. The more they learn, the stronger their skills become.
- **Offer Peer Support**: If they are in a group conflict, volunteer to be a neutral observer or help them find a mediator.

By spreading these tools, you multiply peace around you. Each person who gains conflict resolution ability can then influence more people, creating a ripple effect in society.

## 13. Knowing When to Part Ways

Despite all efforts, some conflicts might persist because the individuals or groups have fundamentally incompatible values or goals, or one side refuses to engage fairly. In rare but real cases:

- **Continued Harm**: If the conflict is abusive or dangerous and the other side will not change, it might be best to leave.
- **Unwillingness to Respect Boundaries**: If you set clear boundaries and they keep violating them, staying might only cause further stress or harm.
- **Incompatible Core Beliefs**: Some differences are so profound that you can maintain a polite relationship but cannot collaborate closely.
- **Toxic Patterns**: If repeated attempts at resolution fail and the environment remains toxic, you may choose to step away for your well-being.

Walking away is not always a failure—it can be self-care or a wise choice when resolution is blocked. You can still apply conflict resolution with others willing to engage.

---

## 14. Technology and the Future of Conflict Resolution

As society grows more connected, new forms of conflict arise—cyberbullying, online harassment, or misunderstandings in global teams. However, the fundamentals you learned still apply:

- **Use Calm Communication**: Whether face to face or digital, respectful language and empathy are crucial.
- **Filter Out Noise**: Online spaces can contain trolls or provocations. Recognizing them and staying above them helps you keep your composure.
- **Verify Information**: Rumors spread quickly online. Before reacting in anger, check sources.
- **Adopt Digital Tools Wisely**: Virtual mediation sessions, group chats with moderators, or AI-based conflict resolution tools might become common. Knowing how to apply them effectively keeps you prepared.
- **Balance Online and Offline**: Face-to-face talks can still solve deep conflicts better than endless texting. Technology is a tool, not a substitute for human empathy.

As the digital era continues, the ability to adapt your conflict resolution methods to virtual platforms ensures you remain effective in bridging differences across wide distances.

## 15. Continual Self-Reflection and Improvement

Conflict resolution is not a one-time lesson. It is a lifelong set of habits. Regular self-reflection helps you keep improving:

1. **Routine Check**: Every month or so, ask, "Have I faced any conflicts recently? How did I handle them? What can I do better next time?"
2. **Set Personal Goals**: Maybe you want to practice deeper listening or learn advanced negotiation techniques.
3. **Stay Updated**: Books, articles, and new research on communication or psychology can offer fresh insights.
4. **Assess Emotional Health**: If you are going through stress, sadness, or anxiety, it can affect how you handle conflict. Taking care of your mental well-being helps you remain calm in disagreements.
5. **Ask for Feedback**: Friends or family might notice things you miss. A simple question like, "During our last conflict, was there anything I could have done better?" fosters growth.

No matter how skilled you become, there is always more to learn. Each new conflict holds lessons, and each reflection improves your ability to address the next one.

## 16. Staying Grounded in Your Values

Conflict resolution is not about pleasing everyone or giving up your core beliefs. Instead, it is about expressing yourself in ways that respect both your values and the other person's humanity. By staying grounded in your own moral principles:

- **You Remain Consistent**: Even in heated arguments, you do not resort to cruelty or dishonesty. Your integrity stays intact.
- **You Avoid Manipulation**: If the other side tries to pressure you into something that violates your values, you can say no firmly but respectfully.

- **You Gain Respect**: People often trust those who hold a stable moral stance without attacking others.
- **You Feel Inner Peace**: Even if conflicts do not resolve perfectly, you know you acted in line with your ethics, reducing regret.

Balancing personal convictions with open-mindedness is a hallmark of advanced conflict resolution. It allows respectful dialogue without self-betrayal.

---

## 17. Diversity of Thought

One reason conflict arises is that different people see the world in unique ways. This can be a gift. By embracing varied opinions, you can:

1. **Discover Hidden Solutions**: A person from a different background or viewpoint might spot a solution you never considered.
2. **Strengthen Tolerance**: Exposure to different ideas helps you empathize with people you once thought were simply wrong.
3. **Enrich Relationships**: Conversations become deeper and more interesting when not everyone automatically agrees.
4. **Reduce Fear of Disagreement**: As you see how new perspectives enhance your life, you become less defensive about your own opinions.
5. **Foster a Culture of Learning**: Groups that appreciate multiple viewpoints become better problem-solvers and adapt faster to changes.

Maintaining harmony in the midst of diverse thoughts is a testament to strong conflict resolution skills. It shows that the group or individuals can handle friction without suppressing uniqueness.

---

## 18. Recognizing the Bigger Picture

When in conflict, it is easy to get stuck in details: who said what, who messed up a small task. Yet stepping back to see the bigger picture can calm tensions and remind everyone of shared goals:

- **In Family Conflicts**: The bigger picture might be the desire to stay connected and caring for each other's well-being.

- **In School Settings**: The main aim is often learning and growth, not personal battles.
- **In Workplaces**: The overarching goal is completing projects, serving clients, or advancing a mission.
- **In Communities**: People generally want a safe, pleasant neighborhood, even if they disagree on how to achieve it.

By refocusing on these broader aims, sides in a conflict can reframe the dispute from "us vs. them" to "how do we fulfill our shared purpose?" That shift often opens fresh avenues for peaceful resolution.

---

## 19. Your Ongoing Responsibility

Having conflict resolution knowledge places a responsibility on you to use it wisely. Even if others resort to rude words or try to provoke you, you can choose a calmer path. This is not always easy:

- **Lead by Example**: When tension flares, demonstrate respectful language and a willingness to listen. Others might follow suit, even if grudgingly at first.
- **Know Your Limits**: Keep self-care in mind. If a conflict is too draining, you might need a break or external support.
- **Offer Help**: Sometimes, you can step in as a neutral friend or colleague if you see two people locked in a conflict, guiding them through calm talk.
- **Stay Humble**: Even skilled peacemakers can lose their cool occasionally. Apologize if you slip, reaffirm your commitment to better practices, and move on.
- **Encourage a Shared Culture**: Suggest to your group or family that you all adopt the same conflict guidelines. Many hands make light work. If everyone supports these principles, it becomes easier to maintain harmony.

Your consistent effort, combined with patience and empathy, can shape the environment around you in positive ways.

## 20. Conclusion

Conflict resolution is an ongoing journey—one that never truly ends. Each new situation or relationship can pose fresh challenges, test your self-control, and expand your ability to listen, empathize, and compromise. The tools you have learned—staying calm, identifying real issues, speaking and listening respectfully, seeking third-party support, and embracing the possibility of growth—will serve you well wherever you go.

When you see conflict as a normal part of life, you become less fearful of disagreements and more curious about what can be learned. By applying self-awareness, empathy, and structured dialogue, you build a pattern of handling problems before they become unmanageable. Over time, this pattern can spread from you to your family, your friends, your coworkers, and your broader community.

Of course, there is no guarantee every conflict will have a neat resolution. Sometimes, the other person might refuse to cooperate, or deeper issues might take a long time to unravel. Yet, your consistent practice of respectful communication sets a tone that others may eventually adopt. Even if a specific conflict remains partly unresolved, you maintain your integrity and keep doors open for possible future conversations.

Going forward, keep refining your skills. Check in with yourself about your emotional state, your triggers, and your growth areas. Learn from each conflict, whether you handle it well or struggle through it. Seek feedback and fresh perspectives. Whenever you need help, do not hesitate to reach out to friends, mediators, or professionals. Conflict resolution is not about solitary heroics—it is about collaboration and empathy.

By continuing these habits, you help create homes that feel safe to share honest feelings, workplaces that solve problems with dialogue instead of office politics, schools that nurture understanding among students, and communities that adapt to challenges through open discussion. You contribute to a society where people do not run from conflict or turn it into aggression, but rather approach it as a chance to make things better.

Thank you for exploring these chapters. The knowledge you have gained can become a strong foundation for living with less fear of conflict and more confidence in your ability to shape respectful, caring relationships. Remember that each time you face a disagreement—big or small—you have a toolbox: calm yourself, ask good questions, use "I" statements, look for shared interests, brainstorm creative solutions, and follow up to ensure lasting improvement.

With these approaches, you will be well-equipped to foster ongoing harmony in your own life and in the groups that matter to you. Conflict might still arise, but now you can meet it not with dread, but with a readiness to discover better outcomes for everyone involved.

www.ingramcontent.com/pod-product-compliance
Lightning Source LLC
LaVergne TN
LVHW012042070526
838202LV00056B/5572